Grim the collier of Croydon.
1662 – Primary Source Edition

William Haughton, John Tatham

The Tudor Facsimile Texts

Grim the Collier of Croydon

The Tudor Facsimile Texts

Under the Supervision and Editorship of

JOHN S. FARMER

Grim the Collier of Croydon

1662

Issued for Subscribers by the Editor of

THE TUDOR FACSIMILE TEXTS
MCMXII

Grim the Collier of Croydon

1662

This play is reproduced from an original now in the British Museum; copies of the play are exceedingly scarce, and they occur only in a collection with the following title:—

> *Gratiæ Theatrales, or A choice Ternary of English plays, Composed upon especial occasions by several ingenious persons; . . Grim the Collier of Croydon, or The Devil and his Dame, with the Devil and St Dunstan a Comedy, by I T Never before published . but now printed at the request of sundry ingenious friends R D 1662 12mo*

As regards this play I have pointed out, in another place, that great uncertainty exists as to date. The probability is that it is a Restoration play founded on an older one, recognisable by such traces as "the plains of new America" (p. 16) and similar allusions.

The "I. T." of the title-page was an adaptor, who, I strongly suspect, was John Tatham (1632-64) and who succeeded John Taylor and Thomas Heywood in the office of laureate to the Lord Mayor's Shows. He was thus largely concerned in stagecraft, and was otherwise engaged in revising plays besides preparing pageants. The play is doubtless very old, but the Seventeenth Century adaptor adapted "without restrictions." As regards authorship Collier suggests Edwards; Fley, William Haughton For the rest, the play is choked with anachronisms; Fulwell's "Like to Like" should be borne in mind. Finally, I must personally explain that the presentment here made of the facsimile is due to the obvious desirability of introducing no new sizes into this series, and "Grim" with one exception—Brandon's "Virtuous Octavia," a 12mo—stands alone as regards size.

The B.M. example lacks the prologue. This I shall give, from the Bodley copy, in one of the volumes of "Dramatic Fragments."

The reproduction of this play from the original is equal in every respect to the standard attained in this series of facsimiles; there is little, if anything, to find fault with

JOHN S. FARMER

GRIM

The Collier of Croyden;

OR,

The Devil and his Dame:

WITH

The Devil and Saint Dunston.

By I. T.

LONDON, Printed in the year, 1662

The Actors Names.

St. *Dunston*, Abbot of *Glassenbury*.
Morgan, Earle of *London*.
Lacy, Earle of *Kent*.
Honorea, *Morgan*'s Daughter.
Marian, her Waiting maid.
Nan, *Marian*'s Maid.
Musgrave, a young Gentleman.
Captain *Clinton*.
Miles Forrest, a Gentleman.
Ralph Harvie, an Apothecary.
Grim, the Collier of *Croyden*.
Parson *Short-hose*.
Clack, a Miller.
Joan, a Country Mayd.
Pluto
Minos.
Æacus.
Rhadamantus.   } Devils.
Belphagor.
Akercock, or *Robin Good-fellow*.
Malbecco his Ghost.
Officers, Attendants, &c.

The Stage is *England*.

(3)

Grim the Collier of *Croydon*.

Actus primus, Scæna prima.

A place being provided for the Devils Consistory, enter
S. Dunstan with his Beads, Book, and
Crosier staff, &c.

S. Dunst. E Nvy that alwayes waits on Vertu's
trayn,
And tears the Graves of quiet sleeping Souls,
Hath brought me, after many hundred years,
To shew my self again upon the earth.
Know then (who list, that I am *English* born,
My name is *Dunston*; whilst I lived with men,
Chief Primate of the Holy *English* Church:
I was begotten in *West Saxony*:
My Fathers name was *Heorston*, my Mothers *Gi-*
nsted.
Endowed with my Metir's legacy,
I stout stir'd in the reign of Seven great Kings;
The first was *Adelstane,* whose Neece *Elfleda*
Malicious tongues reported, I defiled;
Next him came *Edmond*, then *Edred*, and *Edwin* :
And after him reign'd *Edgar,* a great Prince,
But full of many Crimes which I restrain'd :
Edward his son, and lastly *Egelred.*
With all these Kings was I in high esteem,

G 2   And

GRIM THE COLLIER

4

And kept both them, and all the Land in awe;
And, had I liv'd, the *Danes* had never boasted
Their then beginning Conquest of this Land;
Yet some accuse me for a Conjurer,
By reason of those many miracles
Which Heaven for holy life endowed me with.
But who so looks into the golden Legend,
(That sacred Register of holy Saints)
Shall find me by the Pope canoniz'd,
And happily the cause of this Report
Might rise by reason of a Vision,
Which I beheld in great King *Edgar*'s dayes,
Being that time Abbot of *Glastenbury,*
Which (for it was a matter of some worth)
I did make known to few, untill this day :
But now I purpose that the World shall see
How much those Slanderers have wronged me;
Nor will I trouble you with Courts and Kings,
Or drive a feined Battel out of breath ;
Or keep a coyle my self upon the Stage;
But think you see me in my secret cell,
P Arm'd with my Tortass, bidding of my Beads,
But on a sudden I'me o'recome with sleep !
If ought ensue, watch you, for *Dunston* dreams.

He lyeth him down to sleep; Lightning and Thunder;
the Curtains drawn, on a sudden Pluto, Minos,
Æacus, Rhadamantus *set in Counsell, be-*
fore them Malbecco *his Ghost guarded with*
Furies.

Pluto. You ever dreaded Iudges of black Hell,
Grim *Minos,* Æacus, *and* Rhadamant,
Lords of *Cocitus, Styx,* and *Phlegiton,*
Prince, of *Darkness, Pluto's* Ministers,
Know that the greatness of his present Cause
Hath

Hath made our self in person set as judge,
To hear the arraignment of *Malbecco's* Ghost;
Stand forth thou gastly pattern of Despair,
And to this powerfull Synod tell thy tayle,
That we may hear if thou canst justly say
Thou wert not Author of thy own decay.

Malb. Infernal *Iove*, great Prince of *Tartary*,
With humble reverence poor *Malbecco* speaks
Still trembling with the fatal memory
Of his so late concluded Tragedy.
I was (with thanks to your great bounty) bred
A wealthy Lord, whilst that I liv'd on Earth;
And so might have continued to this day,
Had not that plague of mankind faln on me:
For I (poor man) joyn'd woe unto my name,
By choosing out a Woman for my Wife.
A Wife! a curse ordained for the World.
Fair *Hellena!* fair she was indeed,
But fouly stain'd with inward wickedness.
I kept her bravely, and I loved her dear;
But that dear love did cost my Life, and all.
To reckon up a thousand of her pranks,
Her pride, her wastfull spending, her unkindness,
Her false dissembling, seeming sanctity,
Her scolding, powting, prating, meddling,
And twenty hundred more of the same stamp,
Were but to reap an endless Catalogue
Of what the World is plagu'd with every day.
But for the main of that I have to tell,
It chanced thus: Late in a rainy night
A crew of Gallants came unto my House,
And (Will I, Nill I) would forsooth be lodg'd;
I brought them in, and made them all good cheat,
(Such as I had in store) and lodg'd them soft:
Amongst them one, ecclepped *Paridell,*

G 3   (The

(The falsest Thief that ever trod on ground)
Rob'd me, and with him stole away my Wife.
I (for I loved her dear) pursu'd the Thief.
And, after many daies in travel spent,
Found her amongst a crew of Satyrs wilde,
Kissing, and colling all the live-long night:
I spake her fair, and pray'd her to return:
But she in scorn commands me to be gone;
And glad I was to fly, to save my life.
But when I backward came unto my House,
I find it spoyled and all my treasure gone.
Desp'rate and mad, I ran I knew not whither,
Calling and crying out on Heaven, and Fate,
Till seeing none to pity my distress,
I threw my self down head-long on a Rock,
And so concluded all my ills at once.
Now, judge you, *Justice Benchers,* if my Wife
Were not the instrument to end my life.

Pluto. Can it be possible (you Lords of Hell)
Malbecco's tale of Women should be true;
Is Marriage now become so great a Curse,
That Whilome was the comfort of the World?

Minos. Women, it seems, have lost their native shame,
As no man better may complain than I,
Though not of any whom I made my Wife,
But of my Daughter who procur'd my fall.

Æacus. 'Tis strange what Plaints are brought us every day
Of men made miserable by marriage;
So that amongst a thousand, scarcely ten
Have not some grievous actions 'gainst their Wives.

Rhad. My Lord, if *Rhadamant* might counsell you,
Your Grace should send some one into the World,

                                         That

That might make proof if it be true or no.

Plut. And wisely hast thou counselled *Rha.*
Call in *Belphager* to me presently. (*damant,*
    One of the Furies goes for Belphagor.
He is the fittest that I know in Hell
To undertake a task of such import,
For he is patient, mild, and pittifull:
Humours but ill agrees with our King dom.

        Enter Belphagor.
And here he comes; *Belphagor,* so it is,
We in our awfull Synod have decreed,
(Upon occasions to our selves best known)
That thou from hence shalt go into the world,
And take upon thee the shape of a man;
In which estate thou shalt be married:
Choose thee a Wife that best may please thy self,
And live with her a twelvemonth and a day;
Thou shalt be subject unto humane chance
So far as common wit cannot relieve thee;
Thou shalt, of us receive ten thousand pounds,
Sufficient stock to use for thy increase;
But whatsoever happens in that time,
Look not from us for succour or relief;
This shalt thou do, and when the time's expired,
Bring word to us what thou hast seen and done.

    Bel. With all my heart (my Lord) I am con-
So I may have my Servant *Akercock.* (sent,
To wait upon me as if he were my man,
That he may witness likewise what is done.

    Plu. We are contented, he shall go with thee
    Mi. But what meantime decrees your Ma-
        jesty of poor *Malbecco* ?

    Plu. He shall rest with us
Untill *Belphagor* do return again,
And as he finds, so will we give his doom.
Come let us go and set our Spyal forth.

        G 4   Who

Who for a time must make experiment,
If Hell be not on Earth, as well as here. *Exeunt.*

    It thunders and lightens; the Devils go forth;
    Dunston rising, runneth about the Stage,
    laying about him with his Staff.

    Dun. Sathan avaunt, thou art mans enemy,
Thou shalt not live amongst us so unseen,
So to betray us to the Prince of Darkness:
Sathan avaunt, I do conjure thee hence. (deed.
What dream'st thou *Dunston* ? yea I dreamt in-
Must then the Devil come into the world ?
Such is belike the infernal Kings decree;
Well, be it so, for *Dunston* is content,
Mark well the process of the Devil's disguise,
Who happily may learn you to be wise.
Women beware, and make your bargains well,
The Devil, to choose a Wife, is come from hell.
                                        Exit.

        SCENE 2d.

Enter Morgan Earl of London, Lacy *Earl*
of Kent, with Miles Forrest.

    Mor. My Lord of *Kent*, your Honor knows
        my mind,
That ever have, and still do honour you,
Accounting it my Daughter's happiness,
(Amidst her other infelicities)
That you vouchsafe to love her as you do:
How gladly I would grant your Lordships suite,
The Heavens can witness, which with ruthless
    eares
Have often heard my yet unpittied Plaints;

                                        And

And could I find some means for her recovery,
None but your self should have her to your
Wife,
Lacy. My Lord of *London,* now long time it is
Since *Lacy* first was suiter to your Daughter,
The fairest *Honorea,* in whose eyes
Honor it self in Love's sweet bosome lyes:
What shall we say, or seem to strive with heaven,
Who speechless sent her first into the world;
In vain it is for us to think to loose
That which by Natures selfe we see is bound:
Her beauty, with her other vertues joyn'd,
Are gifts sufficient, though shewant a tongue;
And some will count it Vertue in a woman
Still to be bound to un-offending Silence;
Though I could wish with half of all my Lands,
That she could speak: but since it may not be,
'Twere vain to imprison Beauty with her speech.
For. Have you not heard (my Lords) the
wondrous fame
Of holy *Dunston,* Abbot of *Glassenbury,*
What miracles he hath archieved of late,
And how the rood of *Devercott* did speak,
Confirming his opinion to be true,
And how the holy Consistory fell.
Withall the Monks that were assembled there,
Saving one beam, whereon this *Dunston* sate,
And other more such miracles as these.
They say he is of such religious life,
That Angels often use to talk with him,
And tell to him the secrets of the Heavens.
No question, if your Honors would but try,
He could procure my Lady for to speak.
Mor. Believe me *Forrest,* thou hast well advised,
For I have heard of so much talk of him
Lacy. Is not that *Dunston* he, who check'd the

King.   G 5   About.

About his privy dealing with the Nun,
And made him to do pennance for the fault?
Mor. The same is he, for whom I streight will
Miles Forrest shall in poste to *Glassenbury,* (send
And gently pray the Abbot for my sake
To come to *London:* sure I hope the Heavens
Have ordan'd *Dunston* to do Magn good.
Lacy. Let us dispatch him thither presently,
For I my self will stay for his return.
And see some end or other ere I go.
Mor. Come then Lord *Lacy, Forrest* come away.
                                        Exeunt.

SCENE 3d.

Enter Belphagor *attired like a* Physician;
Akercock *his man in a Tawny Coat.*

Bel. Now is *Belphagor* an incarnate Devil,
Come to the earth to seek him out a Dame:
Hell be my speed, and so I hope it will.
In lovely *London* are we here arrived
Whereas I hear the Earl hath a fair Daughter
So full of vertue, and soft modesty,
That yet she never gave a man soul word.
Ak. Marry indeed they say she cannot speak.
Bel. For this cause have I taken this disguise,
And will profess me a Physician,
Come upon purpose for to cure the Lady;
Marry no way shall bind me but her self,
And she I do intend shall be my wife.
Ak. But Master, tell me one thing by the way,
Do you not mean that I shall marry too?
Bel. No *Akercock,* thou shalt be still unwed,
For if they be as bad as is reported,
One wife will be enough to tire us both.

                                        Ak. O

Ak. O then you mean that I shall now and
then,

Have, as it were a course at base with her.

Bel. Nor so, nor so, that's one of Marriage-
plagues,

Which I must seek to shun amongst the rest,
And live in sweet contentment with my wife,
That when I back again return to hell
All women may be bound to reverence me,
For saving of their Credits as I will.
But who comes here?   Enter Capt. *Climon.*

Clin. This needs must tickle *Musgrave* to the
quick,

And stretch his heart-strings farther by an inch,
That *Lucy* must be married to his Love;
And by that Match my marker is near marr'd,
For *Mariana*, whom I most affect;
But I must cast about by some devise
To help my self and to prevent the Earle.

Bel. This Fellow fitly comes to meet with me,
Who seems to be acquainted with the Earle;
Good Fortune guide you Sir.

Cli. As much to you.

Bel. Might I intreat a favour at your hands?

Cli. What's that?

Bel. I am a stranger here in *England*, Sir,
Brought from my native home upon report,
That the Earle's Daughter wants the use of
speech,

I have been practised in such Cures ere now,
And willingly would try my skill on her:
Let me request you so to favour me,
As to direct me to her Father's house.   be

Cli. With all my heart, and welcome shall you
To that good Earle, who mourns his Daughter's want;

But

But they have for a holy Abbot sent,
Who can (men say) do many miracles,
In hope that he will work this wond'rous cure.

Bel. What ere he be, I know 'tis past his skill,
Nor any in the world, besides my self,
Did ever sound the depth of that devise.

Enter Musgrave.

Cli. Musgrave well met; I needs must speak
Musg. I came to seek you.   (with you.

Cli. Tarry you a while.

Shall I intreat you sir to walk before
With this same Gentleman, and overtake you.

Exeunt Bel. Ak.

This is the newes, the Earle of *Kent* is come,
And in all hast the marriage must be made,
Your Lady weeps, and knows not what to do,
But hopes that you will work some means or
other

To stoppe the crosse proceedings of the Earle.

Musg. Alas poor *Clinton*, what can *Musgrave* do?
Unless I should by stealth convey her thence,
On which a thousand dangers do depend.

Cli. Well (to be brief, because I cannot stay)
Thus stands the case, if you will promise me,
To work your Cosen *Marian* to be mine;
I'le so devise that you shall purchase her,
And therefore tell me if you like the match?

Musg. With all my heart Sir, yea and thank
you too.

Cli. Then say no more but leave the rest to me,
For I have plotted how it shall be done;
I must go follow yon fair Gentleman,
On whom I build my hopes. *Musgrave* adue.

Musg. Clinton farewell, I'le wish thee good suc-
cess.   Exeunt.

SCENE

SCENE IV.

Enter Morgan, Lacy, Dunston, Forrest,
Honorea, Marian.

Mor. Thou holy man, to whom the higher Powers,
Have given the gift of Cures beyond conceit;
Welcome thou art unto Earl *Morgans* house!
The house of sorrow yet, unless by thee
Our joyes may spring anew, which if they do,
Reward and praise shall both attend on thee.

Lacy And we will ever reverence thy name,
Making the Chronicles to speak thy praises;
So *Honorea* may but have her speech.

Dun. My Lords, you know the hallowed gifts of Tongues,
Comes from the self-same power that gives us breath.
He binds and looseth them at his dispose,
And in his name will *Dunston* undertake
To work this cure upon fair *Honorea*,
Hang there my Harp, my solitary muse,
Companion of my Contemplation.

He hangs his Harp on the wall.

And, Lady, kneel with me upon the earth,
That both our Prayers may ascend to Heaven.

They kneel down, then enters Clinton, *with*
Belphagor, terming himself Castiliano,
and Akercock *as* Robin Goodfellow.

Clin. So shall you do the Lady a good turn,
And bind both him and me to you for ever.

Bel. I

Bel. I have determin'd what I mean to do.
Clin. Here be the Earles; and with them is the
Bel. What is he praying? Fryer,
Cli. So me thinks he is;
But I'le disturb him, by your leave my Lords,
Here is a Stranger from beyond the Seas
Will undertake to cure your Lordships daughter.

Marg. The holy Abbot is about the cure,
Bel. Yea, but my Lord hee'l never finish it.
Mor. How canst thou tell, what Country-man
Bel. I am by birth, my Lord, a *Spaniard* born,
And by descent came of a Noble house,
Though for the love I bare to secret Arts,
I never car'd to seek for vain Estate,
Yet by my skill I have increased my wealth;
My name *Castiliano*, and my birth
No baser than the best blood of *Casterle*.
Hearing your Daughter's strange infirmity,
Joyn'd with such matchless beauty and rare ver-
I cross'd the Seas on purpose for her good (tue,

Dun. Fond man presuming on thy weaker skill,
That thinkest by Art to over-rule the Heavens:
Thou know'st not what it is thou undertak'st.
No, no, my Lord, your daughter must be cur'd
By fasting, prayer, and religious works;
My self for her will sing a solemn mass,
And give her three sips of the holy Challice,
And turn my Beads with Aves and with Creeds,
And thus, my Lord, your Daughter must be help'd.

Cuf. Zownds, what a prating keeps the bald-pate Fryer?
My Lord, my Lord, here's Church work for an age!
Tush, I will cure her in a minutes space,
That she shall speak as plain as you or I.

Dunston's

Dunstan's Harp sounds on the wall.

Fir. Hark, hark my Lord, the holy Abbot's Harp
Sounds by it self so hanging on the wall?

Dun. Unhallowed man, that scorn'st the sacred reed,
Hark how the testimony of my truth
Sounds heaven'ly musick with an Angel's hand,
To testifi Dunston's integrity.
And prove hy active boast of no effect.

C.f. Tush Sir, that musick was to w l'om me;
The Harp hath not an other Master new,
I warran you 'twill never tune you more.

Dun Who should be Master of my Harp but I?

Cas. Try then what service i will do for you.

He tryes to play, but cannot.

Dun. Thou art some Sorcerer, or Nigromancer,
Who by thy Spells dost hold these holy strings.

Cas Cannot your Ho'yness unbind the bonds?
Then I perceive my skill is most of force;
You see, my Lord, the Abbot is but weak,
I am the man must do your Daughter good.

M r. What wilt thou ask for to work thy cure?

Cas. That without which I will not do the Cure;
Her self to be my Wife, for which intent
I came from *Spain*: then if she shall be mine,
Say so, or keep her else for ever dum.

Mor. The Earle of *Kent*, mine honourable friend,
Hath to my Daughter been a Suiter long,
And much it would displease both her and him
To be prevented of their wished love;
Ask what thou wilt beside, and I will grant it.

                                   Cas. Alass

Cas. Alass my Lord, what should the crazy Earle
Do with so young a Virgin as your Daughter?
I dare stand to her choyce 'twixt him and me.

Lacy. And I will pawn mine Earldome with my Love,
And loose them both, if I loose *Honorea*.

Cas A match my Lords, wee'l stand unto the Choyce.

Mor. I am contented, if the Earle be pleased.

Lacy. I were not worthy of her did I doubt.

Cas Then there it goes, fetch me a bowle of Wine,
This is the match my Lord, before I work,
If she refuse the Earle, she must be mine.

Mor. It is

One brings him a Cup of Wine, he straynes the jayce of the Herb into it.

Cas. Now shall your Lordships see a *Spaniard's*
Who from the plains of new *America*   (skill.
Can find out sacred Symples of esteem
To bind, and unbind Nature's strongest Powers:
This Herb, which mortal men have seldome found,
Can I with ease procure me when I list;
And by this juyce shall *Honorea* speak;
Here Lady, drink the freedom of thy heart,
And may it teach thee long to call me Love.
                                   She drinks.

Now lovely *Honorea* thou art free,
Let thy Celestial voyce make choyce of me.

Hen. Base Alien, mercinary Fugitive,
Presumptuous *Spaniard*, that with shamelofs pride
                                   Dar'st.

Dar'ft ask an Englifh Lady for thy Wife.
I fcorn, my flave fhould honour thee, fo much,
And for my felf, I l ke my felf the worfe,
That thou dar'ft hope the gaining of my Love,
Go, get thee gone, the fhame of my efteem,
And feek fome drudge that may be like thy felf.
But as for you, good Earle of *Kent*,
Me thinks your Lordfhip being of thefe years
Should be paft dreaming of a fecond Wife.
Fy, fy, fy, my Lord, 'ti luft in doting age;
I will not patronize fo foul a fin.
An old man dote on youth I'tis monftrous;
Go, home go home, and reft your Weary head,
'Twere pity fuch a brow fhould learn to bud.
And laftly unto you my Lord, and Father,
Your love to me is too much overfeen,
That in your eare and counfell fhould devife,
To tye your Daughter's choyce to two fuch
      Grooms.
You may elect for me, but I'le difpofe
And fit my felf far better than both thofe;
And fo I will conclude, you as you pleafe.
                    Exit Honorea *in a chafe.*

 Rob. Call you this making of a Woman fpeak?
I think they all wifh fhe were dumb again.
 Caft. How now my Lord, what are you in a
      mufe?
 Lacy. I would to God her Tongue were tyed
      again.
 Caft. I marry Sir, but that's an other thing,
The Devil cannot tye a woman's tongue,
I would the Fryer could do that with his Beads.
But 'tis no matter, you my Lord have promis'd,
If fhe refufe the Earl, fhe fhould be mine.
 Mer. Win her, and wear her man with all my
      heart.
                                    Caft. Oh!

 Caft. Oh! I'le haunt her till I make her ftoop,
Come, come my Lord, This was to try her
      voyce,
Let's in and court her; one of us fhall fpeed.
 Rob. Happy man be his dole that miffeth her,
      fay I.
 Dunft. My weaker Senfes cannot apprehend
The means this Stranger us'd to make her fpeak;
There is fome fecret myftery therein,   (veal,
Conceal'd from *Dunfton* I which the Heavens re-
That may fcourge this bold blafpheming man,
Who holds religious works f little worth.
             Exeunt, manet Clinton *and* Forreft.
 For. Now Captain *Clinton* what think you of
      me?
 Clin. My thinks, as yet, the jeft holds pretty
The one hath taught her to deny himfelf,
The other who'd fo long he cannot fpeed,
 For. This newes will pleafe young *Mufgrave,*
 Clin. Marry will it,
And I will haften to acquaint him with them,
Come let's away.   *Exeunt.*

      Enter Parfon Shorthoufe, *and* Grim *the*
           Collier.

 Grim No, Mr. Parfon, grief hath made my
heart and me a pair of Ballance, as heavy as lead;
every night I dream I am a town top, and that I
am whipt up and down with the fcourge-ftick of
Love, and the mettell of Affection; and when I
work, I find my felf ftark naked and as cold
as a ftone: now judge how I am tumbled
and toft; poor *Grim the Collier* hath wifht himfelf
burnt up amongft his Coles.
                                 Par. Shorth. O

Par. Sforth. O *Grim* be wife dream not of Love
Thy forrows cannot Fancy move,
If *Iug* love thee, love her again;
If not thy kindneff then refrain.

Grim. I am not skill'd in your rhyming Mr.
Parfon ; but that which is bred in the Flefh will
never out of the Bone ; I have feen as much as
another man, my travel fhould teach me, there's
never a day in the Week but I carry Cole from
Croydon to *London*; and now when I rife in the
morning to harnife my Horfes, and load my
Cart, methinks I have a Tayler fewing ftitches
in my Heart ; when I am driving my Cart, my
Heart that wanders one way my Eyes they leere
another, my Feet they lead me I know not whither, but now and then into a Slow over head
and ears; fo that poor *Grim* that before was over
fhooes in Love, is now over head and ears in
Durt and Mire.

Par. Sher. Well *Grim* my counfell fhall fuffice
To help thee, but in any wife
Be rul'd by me, and thou fhall fee,
As thou loveft her, fhe fhall love thee.

Grim. A lar'd ! but do you think that will be
fo, I fhould laugh till I tickle to fee that day, and
forfwear fleep all the next night after ; Oh Mafter Parfon, I am fo haltred in affection, that I
may tell you in fecret, here's no body elfe hears
me, I take no care how I fill my Sacks ; every
time I come to *London* my Coles are found faul-
ty ; I have been five times pilfered, my Coles
given to the Poor, and my Sack burnt before
my face. It were a fhame to fpeak this, but
Truth will come to light ; O *Ione* I thou haft
thrown the Cole-duft of thy love into my eyes
and ftricken me quite blind.

Sherth. Now

Par. Sherth Now afore God the Collier choo-
feth well ;
For beauty, *Iug*, doth bear away the bell :
And I love her ; then Collier thou muft mifs,
For Parfon *Sherth* fe vows, *Iug* fhall be his.
But be rul'd thou *Grim*, I have that in my head,
To plot that how thou fhalt the Maiden wed.

Grim. But are you fure you have that in your
head? O for a hammer to knock that out ; one
blow at your Pate would lay all open to me, and
make me as wife as you.

Sherth. Think'ft thou I do fo often look
For nothing on my learned book,
As that I cannot work the feat ;
I warrant 'le the Miller cheat,
And make *Iug* thine, in fpite of him ;
Will this content thee neighbour *Grim*.

Grim Content me ! Ay and fo highly, that if
you do this feat for me, you hire me to you as
one hireth an Oxe or an Afs to ufe to ride, to
fpur, or any thing ; yours to demand, miferable *Grim* ! *Ione's* Handmaid for fo I have cal-
led my felf ever fince laft *May* day, when fhe gave
me her hand to kifs.

Sherth. Well, let's away, and in all haft,
About it e're the day be paft ;
And ever after, if thou haft her,
Acknowledge me to be thy Mafter.

Grim. I woofe Sir ; Come let's away, the beft
drink in *Croydon's* yours, I have it for you, even
a dozen of Iugs to *Iug's* health. *Ex.* both.

Enter Earl *Morgan*, Earl *Lacy*, Mariana.

Mar. My Lord of *Kent*, the latter motion
Doth

Doth bind me to you in a higher degree,
Than all those many favours gone before;
And now the issue of my help relyes
Only on *Mariana's* gentleness,
Who, if she will in such a common good
Put to her helping hand the Match is made.

Lacy. You need not make a doubt of *Marian,*
Whose love unto her Lady were enough;
Besides her Cozens and her own content,
To move her to a greater thing than this.

Mary. My Lords, if ought there be in *Marian,*
That may or pleasure you, or profit her,
Ye shall not need to doubt of my consent.

Mor. Gramercy *Marian,* and indeed the thing
Is, in it self, a matter of no moment:
If it be weighed aright; and therefore this,
Thou know'st the bargain 'twixt me and the
     Doctor.
Concerning Marriage with my only Daughter,
Whom I determin'd that my Lord of *Kent*
Should have espoused; but I see her mind
Is only set upon thy Cozin *Musgrave,*
And in her Marriage to use constraint
Were boot'ess; therefore thus we have devised,
Lord *Lacy* is content to loose his part,
And to resign his Title to young *Musgrave.*
But now the Doctor will not yield his right;
Thus we determin to begin his hopes:
Thou shalt this night be brought unto his bed,
Instead of her, and he shall marry thee,
Musgrave shall have my Daughter, she her will,
And so shall all things sort to our content.

Lacy. And this thou shalt be sure of *Marian,*
The Doctor's wealth will keep thee royally;
Besides, thou shalt be ever near thy Friends,
That will not see thee wrong'd by any man.

                              Say

Say then wilt thou resolve to marry him?

Mar. My Lords, you know I am but young,
The Doctor's fit for one of riper years,
Yet in regard of *Honorea's* good,
My Cozins profit, and all your contents,
I yield my self to be the Doctor's wife.

Morg. 'Tis kindly spoken, gentle *Marian,*
                         Enter *Castiliano.*
But here the Doctor comes.

Lacy. Then I le away,
Lest he suspect ought by my being here.

Morg. Do, and let me alone to close with him.

Cast. May he ne're speak that makes a VVo-
     man speak,
She talks now. sure for all the time that's past,
Her Tongue is like a Scare-crow in a tree,
That clatters still with every puff of winde;
I have so haunted her from place to place,
About the hall, from thence into the parler,
Up to th Chamber, down into the Garden.
And still she railes, and chafes, and scoulds,
As if it were the Sessions day in hell,
Yet will I haunt her with an open mouth,
And never leave her till I force her love me.

Morg. Now, Master Doctor, what a match or
     no.

Cast. A match, quoth you, I think the Devil
     himself
Cannot match her, for if he could, I should.

Morg. Well, be content, 'tis I must work the
     mean.
To make her yield whether she will or no:
My Lord of *Kent* is gone hence in a chase,
And now I purpose that she shall be yours,
Yet to her self unknown, for she shall think
That *Musgrave* is the man, but it shall be you;
                              Seem

Seem you still discontented and no more:
Go *Mariana* call thy Mistriss hither,
Now when she comes, dissemble what you
 know,
And go away, as if you car'd not for her,
So will she be the sooner brought unto it.
                              Exit Mariana.

Castil. My Lord, I thank you for your honest
 care,
And, as I may, will study to requite it.
                    Enter Honorea and Mariana.

But here your Daughter comes : No, no, my
 Lord,
'Tis not for favour I regard nor her,
Your Promise 'tis I challenge, which I'le have;
It was my Bargain No man else should have her,
Not that I love her, but I'le not be wrong'd
By any one, my Lord, and so I leave you.
                              Exit Castil.

Morg. He's passing cunning to deceive him-
But all the better for the after sport.   (self,
Hon. Sir did you send for me.
Morg. Honorea, for thee.
And this it is, how e'e unworthily
I have bestowed my love so long upon thee,
That wilt so manifestly contradict me;
Yet, that thou mav'st perceive how I esteem
I make thy self the Guardian of thy Love, (thee,
That thine own fancy may make choyce for
I have perswaded with my Lord of *Kent*, (thee;
To leave to love thee. Now the peevish Doctor
Swears, that his int'rest he will ne're resign ;
Therefore we must by Policy deceive him,
He shall suppose he lyeth this night with thee,
But *Mariana* shall supply thy room,
And thou with *Musgrave* in another Chamber,
                                        Shalt

Shalt secretly be lodg'd; when this is done,
Twill be too late to call that back again,
So shalt thou have thy mind, and he a wife.
Hon. But wilt thou, *Mariana* yield to this.
Mar. For your sake, Lady I will undertake it.
Hon. Gramercy *Marian*, and my noble Father,
Now I acknowledge that indeed you love me.
Morg. Well, no more words, but be you both
        prepar'd,
The night draweth on, and I have sent in secret
For *Musgrave*, that he may be brought unseen,
To hide suspition from their jealous eyes.
Hon. I warrant you, come *Marian*, let us go.
                          Exeunt Hon. & Mar.

Morg. And then, my Lord of *Kent*, shall be
 my Sonne,
Should I go wed my Daughter to a Boy ?
No, no young Girles must have their Wills re-
strain'd,
For if the Rule be theirs, all runnes to nought.
                                        Exit.

Enter Clack the Miller, with Ione.

Clack. Be not *Iug*, as a man would say, finer
than Five pence, or that it you are more proud
than a Peacock that is, to seem to scorn to call
in at *Clacks* mill as you pass over the bridge,
there be as good Wenches as you be glad to pay
me toll.

Ione Like enough *Clack*, I had as live they as I,
and a great deal rather too ; you that take to I of
so many Maids, shall never toale me after you :
Oh God, what a dangerous thing 'tis but to peep
once into Love! I was never so haunted with
                                        my

my harvest-work as I am with Love's passions.

Clack. I but *Ione*, beat old Proverbs in your membry, soft and fair; now sir, if you make too much haste to fall foul, I and that upon a foul one too, there fades the flower of all *Croydon*, tell me but this, is not *Clack* the Miller as good a name as *Grim* the Collier?

Ione. Alass, I know no difference in names; To make a Maid, or choose, or to refuse.

Clack. You were best to say, No, nor in men nother. Well, I'le be sworn I have; but I have no reason to tell you so much, that care so little for me; yet hark;

Clack speaketh in her ear: enter Grim, *Parson* Shorthose.

Grim. O Mr. Parson, there he stands like a Scare-crow to drive me away from her, that sticks as close to my heart, as my shirt to my back, or my hose to my heel; O Mr. Parson *Shorthose*, *Grim* is but a man as another man is. Colliers have but lives as other men have; all's gone, if she go from me, *Grim* is no body without her, my heart is in my mouth, my mouth is in my hand, my hand threatens vengeance against the Miller, as it were a Beadle with a whip in his hand, triumphing o're a Beggar's back.

Short. Be silent *Grim*, stand close and see, So shall we know how all things be.

Grim. In wisedom I am appeas'd, but in anger I broyle as it were a rasher upon the coles.

Ione. I'le not despise the Trades ye either have, Yet *Grim* the Collier may, if he be wise, Live even as merry as the day is long;

H   For

For, in my judgement, in his mean estate Consists as much content, as in more wealth.

Grim. O Mr. Parson, write down this sweet saying of her in *Grim's* commendations; she hath made my heart leap like a hobby horse; O *Ione* this speech of thine will I carry with me even to my grave.

Short. Be silent then.

Clack. Well, then I perceive you mean to lead your life in a Colepit, like one of the Devil's drudges, and have your face look like the outside of an old iron pot, or a blacking box.

Grim. He calleth my Trade into question, I cannot forbear him.

Short. Nay then you spoyle all neighbour *Grim*, I warrant you she will answer him.

Ione. What I intend I am not bound to shew To thee, nor any other but my Mother, To whom in duty I submit my self; Yet this I tell thee, though my birth be mean, My honest vertuous life shall help to mend it, And if I marry any in all this life, He shall say boldly he hath an honest wife.

Grim. O that 'twere my fortune to light upon her, on that Condition my Horses were dead, and my Cart broken, and I bound to carry Coles as long as I live from *Croydon* to *London* on my bare shoulders; Mr. Parson the Flesh is frayle, he shall tempt her no longer; she is but weak, and he is the stronger; I'le upon him. Miller thou art my neighbour, and therein charity hold my hands; but me thinks you having a water-gapp of your own, you may do as other Millers do, grind your grist at home, knock your coggs into your own Mill. you shall not cogg with her she doth discry thee, and I defie thee to a mortal fight.

fight, and so, Miller, good night. And now
sweet *Ione*, be it openly known thou art my own.

Clark. Well *Grim*, since thou art so Collier-like
chollerick.

Grim. Miller, I will not be mealy mouth'd.

Clark. I'le give thee the fewer words now, be
cause the next time we meet I'le pay thee all in
dry blowes, carry Coles at a Collier's hands?
and I do let my Mill be drown'd up in water, and
I hang'd in the roof.

Ione. And if thou lovest me *Grim*, forbear him
now.

Grim. If I love thee! dost thou doubt of that?
nay ripp me up, and look into my heart, and
thou shalt see thy own face pictur'd there as
plainly as in the proudest Looking glass in all
Croydon; if I love thee! then tears gush out, and
shew my love.

Clark. What Mr. Parson are you there? you
remember you promis'd to win *Ione* for my own
wearing?

Shorr. I warrant thee *Clark*; but now be gone,
Leave me to work that here alone.

Clark. Well, farewell Mr. *Shorthose*, be true
when you are trusted. *Ex Clark.*

Shorr. She shall be neither his nor thine,
For I intend to make her mine,

Grim. If I love thee *Ione*; those very words
are a purgation to me, you shall see desparation
in my face, and death marching in my very
countenance; If I love!

Shorr. What *Grim* hath grief drown'd thee ag
Are all thy joyes over cast? (last?
Is *Ione* in place, and thou so sad,
Her presence, man, should make thee glad.

Ione. Good Master Parson, 'twere no fault of
mine, H2 He

te takes occasion where there none was given;
I will not blab unto the World, my love
I owe to him, and shall do whilst I live.

Grim. Well *Ione*, without all ifs or Ands, E-
persese, A-persese, or Tittle-tattles in the
world, I do love thee, and so much, that in thy
absence I cry when I see thee, and rejoyce with
my very heart when I cannot behold thee.

Shorr. No doubt; no doubt thou lovest her
But listen now to what I tell; (well.
Since ye are both so well agreed,
I wish you make more hast and speed,
To morrow is *Holy-rood* day,
When all a nutting take their way,
Within the Wood a Close doth stand,
Incompast round on either hand,
With Trees and Bushes, there will I
Dispatch your marriage presently.

Grim. O Master Parson, your devising pate
hath blest me for ever; *Ione* we'le have that so;
the shorter the work, the sweeter.

Ione. And if my Mother give but her consent,
My absence shall in no case hinder it.

Grim. Shee! quotha, she is mine already, we'le
to her presently. Mr. Parson; 'tis a match;
we'le meet you: now Miller do I go beyond you,
I have stript him of the Wench, as a Cook would
strip an Eele out of her skin, or a Pudding out of
the Case thereof; now I talk of a Pudding, O
'tis my only food, I am old dog at it; Come *Ione*,
let's away, I'le pudding you.

Shorr. Well, if my Fortune luckily ensue,
As you shall cozen him, I'le cozen you.

Exeunt.

Enter

Enter Castiliano *at one door with* Mariana, *Earle* Lacy, *at an other door with*
Honorea.

Cast. Come lovely *Honorea*, bright as day,
As came *Alcmena* from her sacred bed
With *Iupiter*, shapt like *Amphitrio*:   (here?
So show my Love, my Love! whom have we
Hon. Sweet *Musgrave*; out alas I am betray'd!
Cast. Thou art my Love?
Lacy. No, mine?
Hon. Nor yours, nor yours:
But *Musgrave's* Love; O *Musgrave* where art thou?
    Lacy. Be not displeas'd my Dear, give me thy
        hand.
    Hon. My hand, false Earle, nor hand not heart
        of mine;
Could'st thou thus cunningly deceive my hopes,
And could my Father give consent thereto,
Well, neither he nor thou shalt force my Love.
    Cast. 'Tis I fair *Honorea* am thy Love,
Forsake the worthless Earle, give me thy hand.
    Mari. Whose hand would you have sir? this
        hand is mine,
And mine is yours, then keep you to your own.
    Mari. Yet are you mine, sir, and I mean to
        keep you;
What, do you think to shake me off so soon?
No gentle Husband, now it is too late;
You should have look'd before you came to bed.

Enter Rob. Goodf. *with his Masters Gown.*

Rob. Many good morrows to my gentle Master,   H 3   And

And my new Mistriss, God give you both joy;
What say you to your Gown sir, this cold morn-
        (ing!
    Cast. Robin I am undone, and cast away.
How Master, cast away upon a Wife!
    Cast. Yea Robin cast away upon a Wife.
    Rob. Cast her away then Master; can you not?
    Mar. No, sir he cannot, nor he shall not do it.
    Rob. Why, how knew you? I am sure you
        are not she.
    Mar. Yes sir, I am your Mistriss as it falls.
    Rob. As it falls? quoth ye, marry a foul fall
        is it.
    Mar. Base Rascal, dost thou say that I am foul?
    Rob. No, 'twas foul play for him to fall upon
        you.
    Mar. How know you that he fell, were you so
        nigh.
            She giveth Robin *a box on the ear.*
    Rob. Mass it should seem 'twas he that fell if
        any.
For you me thinks are of a mounting nature;
What, at my Eares at first! a good beginning.
    Lacy. My dear Delight, why dost thou stain
        thy Cheeks?
Those rosie Reds with this unseemly dew;
Shake off those Tears that now untimely fall,
And smile on me, that am thy Summers joy.
    Hon. Hapless am I to loose so sweet a prison,
Thus to obtain a weary liberty;
Happy had I been so to have remain'd,
Of which estate I ne're should have complain'd.
    Rob. Whoop whoo! more Marriages! and all
of a sort; happy are they, I see, that live with-
out them; if this be the beginning, what will be
the ending?
                                        Enter

Enter to them Earle Morg. and Dunst.

Mor. Look *Dunston* where they be, displeas'd
no doubt,
Try if thou canst work reconciliation.

Cast. My Lord, I challenge you of breach of
promise,
And claim your Daughter here to be my wife.

Lacy. Your claim is nought, sir, she is mine
already.

Hon. Your claim is nought Sir, I am none of
yours.

Mar. Your claim is here Sir, *Marian* is yours.
What Husband, newly married, and inconstant!
Greed we so well together all this night,
And must we now fall out? for shame, for shame.
A man of your years, and be so unstayed!
Come, come away, there may no other be,
I will have you, therefore you shall have me.

Rob. This is the bravest Country in the world,
Where men get wives whether they will or no;
I trow e're long some Wench will challenge me.

Cast. Oh! is not this a goodly consequence,
I must have her, because she will have me?

Dunston. Ladies and Gentlemen, here *Dunston*
speak:
Marriage, no doubt, is ordain'd by Providence,
Is sacred, not to be, by vain affect,
Turn'd to the idle humours of mens brains;
Besides, for you my Ladie *Honorea*,
Your durie binds you to obey your Father,
Who better knows what fits you than your self;
And 'twere, in you, great folly to neglect
The Earle's great love, whereof you are unwor-
thy,

H 4   Should

Should you but seem offended with the match;
Therefore submit your self to make amends;
For 'tis your fault, so may you all be friends.

Morg. And Daughter, you must think what
I have done,
Was for your good, to wed you to the Earle,
Who will maintain and love you royally:
For what had *Musgrave* but his idle shape?
A shadow to the substance you must build on.

Rob. She will build substances on him I trow,
Who keeps a shrew against her will, had better
let her go.

Mar. Madam conceal your grief, and seem
content,
For, as it is, you must be rul'd perforce;
Dissemble till convenient time may serve
To think on this dispite and *Musgrave's* love.

Lacy. Tell me my Dear, will thou at length be
pleas'd.

Hon. As good be pleas'd, my Lord, as not be
eas'd;
Yet though my former love did move me much,
Think not amiss, the same love may be yours.

Cast. What! is't a Match? ney then since you
agree,
I cannot mend my self, for ought I see;
And therefore, 'tis as good to be content:
Come Lady, 'tis your lot to be my Dame.
Larding, adieu. God send ye all good speed;
Some have their Wives for pleasure, some for
need.

Lacy. Adieu *Castiliano* we are friends?

Cast. Yes, yes, my Lord, there is no remedy.

Rob. No remedy, my Masters for a Wife?
A note for young beginners, mark it well.

Exeunt all.
Enter

Enter Forrest, *Capt.* Clinton, Harvey.

For. Now Gallants what imagine you of this,
Our notes are all flirts for *Mariana*,
The Spanish Doctor hath her to his wife;
And *Musgraves* hopes are dead for *Honorea*,
For she is married to the Earle of *Kent*,
'Twill be good sport to see them when they rise,
If so they be not gotten up already?
  Clin. I say the Devil go with them all for me,
The Spanish Doctor marry *Marian!*
I think that Slave was born to cross me still;
Had it not been last day before the Earle,
Vpon my Conscience I had crack'd his Crown,
When first he ask'd the Lady for his Wife;
Now hath he got her too, whom I desir'd,
Why, he'le away with her e're long to *Spain*,
And keep her there to dispossess our hopes.
  For. No, I can comfort ye for that suppose;
For yesterday he hir'd a dwelling house,
And here he means to tarry all this year,
So long at least, what e're he doth hereafter.
  Clin. A sudden plot-form comes into my
    minde,
And this it is, *Miles Forrest*, thou and I
Are partly well acquainted with the Doctor,
Ralph Harvey shall along with us to him,
Him we'le prefer so: his Apothecary:
Now, sir, when *Ralph* and he are once acquaint-
His wife may often come unto his House,   (ed,
Either to see his Garden, or such like;
For doubt not Women will have means enough
If they be willing, as I hope she will;
There may we meet her, and let each one plead,
He that speeds best, why let him carry it.
            H 3   *For. I.*

  For. I needs must laugh, to think how all we
    three,
In the contriving of this feat, agree;
But having got her, every man will strive,
How each may other of her love deprive.
  Clin. Tut, *Forrest*, Love admits these friendly
    strifes;
But say, How like you of my late devise?
  For. Surpassing well, but let's about it streight,
Lest he, before our comming be provided.
  Clin. Agreed.   *Exeunt.*

Enter Musgrave *and* Mariana.

  Musg. Tush Cozen, tell not me; but this devise
Was long ago concluded 'twixt you two,
Which divers reasons move me to imagine;
And therefore these are toyes to blind my eyes,
To make me think she only loved me,
And yet is married to another man.
  Mar. Why Cozen *Musgrave*, are your eyes so
    blinde,
You cannot see the truth of that report;
Did you not know my Lord was alwaies bent,
Whatever came, to wed her to the Earle:
And have you not, besides, heard the devise
He us'd to marry her against her will,
Bettay'd, poor soul, unto Earle *Lacy's* bed,
She thought she held young *Musgrave* in her
    armes.
Her morning tears might testifie her thoughts;
Yet thou shalt see she loves thee more than him,
And thou shalt taste the sweets of her delights;
Mean time my House shall be thy mansion,
And thy abode, for thither will she comes
Vse thou that opportunity, and try
                          Whether

Whether she loved thee, or did but dissemble.

Musg. If she continue kind to me hereafter
I shall imagine well of her and you.   *Ent.* Cast.

Cast. Now Dame, in talk, what Gentleman is
this?

Mar. My Cozen *Musgrave*, Husband, comes to
see you.

Cast. *Musgrave!* now on my Faith heartily
welcome:
Give me thy hand, my Cozen, and my Friend,
My Partner in the loss of *Honorea*,   (like:
We two must needs be Friends, our Fortune's
Marry, yet I am richer by a Shrew.

Marian. 'Tis better be a Shrew, sir, then a
Sheep;
You have no cause I hope yet to complain.

Cast. No Dame, for yet you know 'tis honey
moone;
What, we have scarcely setled our acquaintance.

Musg. I doubt not, Cozen, but ye shall agree;
For she is mil'd enough if she be pleas'd.

Cast. So is the Devil, they say, yea Cozen, yea,
My Dear and I, I doubt not, shall agree.
                                Enter Robin.

Rob. Sir, here be two or three Gentlemen at
the door Would gladly speak a word with your
Worship.
            Enter Clinton, Forrest, Harvey.
They need no bidding me thinks, they can come
alone.

Clin. God save you Seignior *Castilians.*

Cast. O Captain *Comesta*, Welcom all my friends.

For. Sir, we are come to bid *God give you joy*,
And see your House.

Mar. Welcome Gentlemen:
'Tis kindely done to come to see us here.

                                        This.

Ro. This kindnesse makes me fear my Master's
head;
Such hot spurs must have game; how e're they
get it.

Clin. We have a suite to you, *Castiliano.*

Cast. What is it. Sir, if it lyes in me, 'tis done.

Clu. Nay, but a trifle Sir, and that is
This same young man, by trade Apothecary,
Is willing to retein unto your Cures.

Castil. Marry with all my heart and welcome
too.
What may I call your name my honest friend?

Har. *Ralph Harvey* Sir, your neighbour here
hard by,
The Goulden Lyon is my dwelling place,
Where what you please shall be with care perform'd.

Cast. Gramercies *Harvey;* welcome all my
Friends,
Let's in and handsell our new mansion house
With a carousing round of Spanish wine.
Come Cozen *Musgrave*, you shall be my Guest,
My Dame, I trow, will welcome you her self.

Marian No Boy, Lord *Lacy's* wife shall welcome thee.

Rob. So now the game begins; here's some
Cheer toward;
I must be Skinker then, let me alone,
They all shall want o're *Robin* shall have none.
                        Exeunt all but Clin. & Harvi

Clin. Sirra, *Ralph Harvey*, now the entry is made,
Thou only hast accesse without suspect,
Be not forgetfull of thy Agent here,
Remember *Clinton* was the man that did it.

Har. Why Captain, now you talk in jealousie.

                                        Do.

Do not misconster my true meaning heart
  Clinton. Ralph. I believe thee, and rely on thee,
Do not too long absent thee from the Doctor;
Go in, carowse, and taynt his Spanish brayne,
I'le follow and my *Marian's* health maintain.
  Har. Captain, you well advise me, i'le go in,
And for my self, my love-suites I'le begin.
                Exeunt.

ACT. III.

Enter Rob. Goodfellow with his head broken

  Rob. The Devil himself take all such Dames
    for me
Zounds, I had rather be in hell than here;
Nay let him be his own man if he list.
Robin means not to stay to be used thus,
The very first day in her angry spleen,
Her nimble hand began to greet my Eares
with such unkind salutes as I ne're felt;
And since that time there hath not past an hour
Wherein she hath not either rayl'd upon me,
Or laid her anger-load upon my limbs;
Even now for no occasion in the world,
But as it pleas'd her Ladiship to take it,
She gave me up a staff and break, my head;
But I'le no longer serve so curs'd a Dame,
I'le run as fast as my leggs will bear me,
What shall I do? to Hell I dare not go!
Untill my Master's Twelve months be expired.
And here to stay with Mistress *Marian,*
Better to be so long in purgatory.
Now farewell Master, but shrewd Dame fare il

I'le leave you, though the Devil is with you
  still.   *Ex.* Robin.

Enter Mariana *alone chafing.*

  Mar. My heart still pants within; I am so
  chaft,
The Rascal slave my man, that sneaking Rogue
Had like to have undone us all for ever;
My Cozen *Musgrave* is with *Honorea,*
Set in an Arbour in the Summer Garden,
And he, forsooth, must needs go in for hearbs,
And told me further, that his Master bid him;
But I laid hold upon my Younker's pate,
And made the blood run down about his ears.
I trow he shall ask me leave ere he go;
Now is my Cozen Master of his Love,
The Lady at one time reveng'd and pleas'd:
So speed they all that marry Maids perforce;
              Enter Castiliano.

But here my Husband comes.
  Cast. What Dame alone?
  Mar. Yes Sir, this once for want of company.
  Cast. Why, where's my Lady, and my Cozen
  Musgrave?
  Mar. You may go look them both for ought I
  know.
  Cast. What; are you angry Dame?
  Mar. Yea, so it seems.
  Cast. What is the cause I prethee?
  Mar. Why would you know?
  Cast. That I might ease it, if it lay in me.
  Mar. O, but it belongs not to your trade.
  Cast. You know not that.
  Mar. I know you love to prate, and so I leave
  you.   *Exit* Mar.   *Cast.* Well,

Cast. VVell, go thy ways; oft have I raked hell
To get a wife, yet never found her like:
VVhy this it is to marrie with a Shrew.
Yet, if it be, as I presume it is,
There's but one thing offends both her and me,
And I am glad if that be it offends her.
'Tis so no doubt, I read it in her brow,
Lord Lacy shall, with all my heart, enjoy
Fair Honorea, Marian is mine,
VVho though she be a Shrew, yet is she honest;
So is not Honorea, for even now,
VValking within my Garden all alone,
She came with Musgrave, stealing closely by,
And follows him that seeks to flye from her,
I spied this all unseen, and left them there;
But sure my Dame hath some conceit thereof,
And therefore she is thus angry, honest Soul.
VVell, I'le streight hence unto my Lord of Kent,
And warn him watch his wife from these close
 meetings.
VVell Marian, thou livest yet free from blame,
Let Ladies go, thou art the Devil's Dame.
     Exit Castill.

Enter the Devil like Musgrave with Honorea.

Musg. No Lady, let thy modest vertuous life,
Be alwaies joined with thy comely shape,
For Lust ecclipseth Nature's ornament.
 Hon. Young heady Boy, think'st thou thou
 shalt recall
Thy long made Love, which thou so oft hast
 sworn?
Making my Maiden-thoughts to dote on thee.
 Musg. With patience hear me, and if what I
say   Shall

Shall jump with reason, then you'l pardon me:
The time hath been when my Soul's libertie
Vow'd servitude unto that heavenly face,
VVhilst both had equal libertie of choice:
But since the holy bond of marriage
Hath left me single, you a wedded wife,
Let me not be the third, unlawfully
To do Earle Lacy so foul Injurie;
But now at last,
 Hon. I would that last
Might be thy last, thou Monster of all men.
 Musg. Hear me with patience.
 Hon. Cease, I'le hear no more;
'Tis my Affection, and not Reason speaks;
Then Musgrave turn the hardness of thy heart,
And now at last incline thy love to mine.
 Mus. Nay now I see thou wilt not be reclaim'd,
Go and bestow this hot love on the Earle,
Let not these loose affects, thus scandalize
Your fair report; go home and learn to live
As chaste as Lucrece, Madam so I leave you.
     She pulleth him back.
 Hon. O stay a little while, and hear my rogue
Speak my hearts words, which cannot choose but
 tell thee,
I hate the Earle, only because I love thee.
     Exit Musgrave.
Musgrave return, hear Honorea speaks:
Disdain hath left him wings to flye from me,
Sweet Love lend me thy wings to overtake him,
For I can stay him with kind dalliance!
All this is but the blindness of my fancy;
Recall thy self: let not thy honour bleed
VVith the foul wounds of Infamie and Shame:
Thy proper Home shall call me home again,
Where my dear Lord bewailes as much as I,
          His

His too much love to her that loves not him.
Let none hereafter fix her maiden love
Too firm on any, lest she feel with me,
Musgrave's revolt, and his unconstancy. *Exit*

Enter Forrest *with* Marian.

For. Tut, I'le remember thee, and streight re-
But heres the Doctor.   turn,
  Mar. Where? *Forrest,* farewell,
I would not have him see me for a world.
  For. Why? he is not here, well now I see you
    fear him.
  Mar. Marry beshrew thee for thy false alarum,
I fear him? no, I neither fear nor love him.
  For. But where's my Lady, she is gone home
    before,
And I must follow after, *Marian* farewell.
  Mar. I shall expect your comming.
  For. Presently, and hearest thou *Marian,* nay it
    shall be so.
                        He whispereth in her ear.
  Mar. O Lord, sir, you are wed I warrant you,
We'le laugh, be merry, and it may be kis,
But if you look for more, you aime amiss.
  For. Go to, go to, we'le talk of this anon.
                        Exit. Forrest.
  Mar. Well go thy way, for the true heartedst
That livest, and as full of honesty,   (man
And yet as wanton as a pretty Lambe:
He'le come again, for he hath loved me long,
And so have many more besides himself:
But I was coy and proud, as Maids are wont,
Meaning to match beyond my mean estate,
Yet have I favoured youths, and youthful
    spotts,   Although

Although I durst not venture on the main;
But now it will not be so soon espy'd.
Maids cannot, but a wife a fault may hide.
                        Enter Nan.

What *Nan?*
  Nan. Anon forsooth.
  Mar. Come hither Maid,
Here take my keyes, and fetch the galley pot,
Bring a fair Napkin, and some fruit dishes,
Dispatch and make all ready presently.
Miles Forrest will come streight to drink with me.
  Nan. I will forsooth.   *Exit* Nan.
  Mar. Why am I young, but to enjoy my years?
Why am I fair, but that I should be loved?
And why should I be loved, and not love other:?
Tut, she is a fool, that her affection smothers:
'Twas not for love I was the Doctor's wife,
Nor did he love me when he first was mine;
Tush, tush, this Wife is but an idle name,
I purpose now to try another Game.
Art thou return'd so soon? O 'tis welldone.
                        Enter Nan *with the Banquet.*
And hearest thou *Nan,* when *Forrest* shall return,
If any happen to enquire for me,
Whether't be Captain *Clinton,* or *Ralph Harvey,*
Call presently, and say thy Master is come,
So I'le send *Forrest* o're the Garden pale.
  Nan. I will forsooth.
  Mar. Mean time stay thou and make our ban-
    quet readie,
I'le to my Closet, and be here again,
Before *Miles Forrest* shall come visit me. *Ex.* Mar.
  Nan. I wonder what my Mistriss is about,
Somewhat she would not have my Master
    know;
What e're it be, it's nothing unto me,
                        She

She is my good Mistriss, and I'le keep her
        Counsell,
I have oft seen her kiss behind his back,
And laugh and toy when he did little think it :
O what a winking eye the Wanton hath
To cozen him, even when he looks upon her.
But what have I to do with what she doth ?
I'le taft her Ionkets, since I am alone,
That which is good for them, cannot hurt me,
I marry this is sweet, a cup of Wine
Will not be hurtfull for disgestion.   *Ent. Caft.*

  Caft. I would I had been wifer once to day,
I went on purpose to my Lord of *Kent*,
To give him some good counsell for his VVife,
And he, poor Heart, no sooner heard my newes,
But turns me up his VVhites, and falls flat down ;
There I was fain to rub and chafe his veins,
And much ado we had to get him live ;
But for all that he is extremely fiek,
And I am come in all the haft I may
For Cordials to keep the Earle alive :
But how now, what a Banquet what means this ?

  Nan. Alass my Master is come home himself ;
Mistriss, Mistriss, my Master is come home,
                              He ftops her mouth.

  Caft. Peace you young Strumpet, or I'le ftop
        your speech :
Come hither Maid, tell me, and tell me true,
VVhat means this Banquet? what's your Miftriss
        doing ?   (comming ?
Why cam'ft thou out, when as thou faw'ft me
Tell me, or elfe I'le hang thee by the heels,
And whip thee naked : come on, what's the mat-
  Nan. Forfooth I cannot tell.   (ter?
  Caft. Can you not tell : come on, I'le make
        you tell me.
  No. O Master, I will tell you.   *Caft.*

  Caft. Then fay on.
  Nan. No thing in truth forfooth but that fhe
        means
To have a Gentleman come drink with her.
  Caft. What Gentleman ?
  Man. Forfooth 'tis Mr. *Forreft* as I think.
  Caft. Forreft ! nay then I know how the Game
        goeth,
Who ever loofeth I am sure to win
By their great kindness, though't be but the
        Hornes :

                    Enter Forreft *at one door,*
                        Marion *at another.*

But here comes he and fhe, come hither Maid,
Upon thy life give not a word, a look,
That fhe may know ought of my being here ;
Stand ftill, and do what e're fhe bids thee do.
Go, get thee gone, but if thou doft betray me,
I'le cut thy Throat, look to it, fot I will do it ;
I'le ftand here clofe to fee the end of this,
And fee what Reaks fhe keeps when I'm abroad.

  Mar. 'Tis kindly done *Miles* to return fo foon,
And fo I take it.   *Nan.* is our Banquet ready ?
Welcome my Love, I fee you'l keep your word.
  Nan. 'Twere better for yee both he had not
        kept it.
  For. Yea *Mariana*, elfe I were unworthy,
I did but bring my Lady to the door,
And there I left her full of melancholly,
And difcontented.
  Mar. Why, 'twas kindly done,
Come, come fit down, and let us laugh a while,
Maid, fill fome Wine
  Nan. Alafs my Breech makes Buttons,
And fo would theirs, knew they as much as I.
                                        He

de may change the sweet meats, and put
urging comfits in the Dishes.

Mar. Here's to my Lady, and my Cozen *Muſ-*
grave.

For. I pray remember gentle Maſter Doctor,
And good Earle *Lazy* too among the reſt.

Caſt. O ſir, we find you kind, we thank you
for it,
The time may come when we may cry you quit,

Nan. Maſter, ſhall I ſteal you a cup of wine?

Caſt. Away you Baggage, hold your peace you
Wretch.

For. But I had rather walk into your Orchard,
And ſee your Gallary ſo much commended,
To view the Workmanſhip he brought from
Spain,
Wherein's deſcrib'd the banquet of the gods.

Mar. I, there's one piece exceeding lively done,
Where *Mars* and *Venus* lye within a net,
Incloſ'd by *Vulcan,* and he looking on.

Caſt. Better and better yet, 'twill mend anon.

Mar. Another of *Diana* with her Nymphes,
Bathing their naked bodies in the ſtreams,
Where fond *Acteon,* for his eyes offence,
Is turn'd into a Hart's ſhape, hornes and all;
And this the Doctor hangs right o're his bed.

For. Thoſe Hornes may fall and light upon his
head.

Caſt. And if they doe, worſe Luck, what remedy?

For. Nay *Marian,* we'le not leave theſe ſights
unſeen,
And then wee'le ſee your Orchard and your
fruit;
For now there hangs Queen apples on the trees,
And one of them are worth a ſcore of theſe.

Mar. Well,

Mar. Well, you ſhall ſee them, leaſt you looſe
your longing.

Exeunt Marian and Forreſt.

Caſt. Nay, if ye fall alonging for green fruit,
Childe-bearing is not far of I am ſure:
Why this is excellent, I feel the buds,
My Head groweth hard, my Horns will ſhortly
ſpring,
Now who may lead the Cuckold's dance but I?
That am become the head man of the Pariſh:
O! this it is to have an honeſt wife,
Of whom ſo much I boaſted once to day.
Come hither Minks, you know your Miſtriſs's
minde,
And you keep ſecret all her villanies,
Tell me, you were beſt. where was this Plot de-
viſed?
How did theſe Villaines know I was abroad?

Nan. Indeed forſooth I knew not when it
was,
My Miſtriſs call'd me from my work of late,
And bad me lay a Napkin; ſo I did,
And made this Banquet ready: but in truth
I knew not what ſhe did intend to do.

Caſt. No, no, you did not watch againſt I
came,
To give her warning to diſpatch her Knaves?
You cryed not out, when as you ſaw me come,
All this is nothing but I'le rouſe you all.

Nan. In truth good Maſter.

Enter Marian, Forreſt,

Caſt. Peace I ſay, they come,
Whimper not, and you do, I'le uſe you worſe:
Behold

Behold that wicked Strumpet with that Knave,
O that I had a pistoll for their sakes,
That at one shot I might dispatch them both :
But I must stand close yet, and see the rest.

Mar. How like'st thou *Miles* my Orchard, and
my House.

For. Well, thou art seated to thy hearts content ;

A pleasant Orchard, and a House well furnisht,
There nothing wants; but in the Gallary
The Painter shews his art exceedingly.

Mar. Yet is there one thing goeth beyond all
these,
Contented life, that giveth the Heart his ease.
And that I want.   *One knocketh at the door.*

For. Sweet Love, adieu.   *Ex. For.*

Mar. Farewell Sweetheart. VVho is that at
the door ?

Clin. A Friend.   *Enter Clinton.*

Mar. Come near. What Captain is it you ?

Clin. Even I, fair *Marian* watching carefully
The blessed step of opportunity.

Mar. Good, good ! how Fortune gluts me
with excess ?
Still they that have enough shall meet with
more.

Clin. But where's the Doctor ?

Mar. Ministring abroad
Physick to some sick Patients he receins.

Clin. Let him abroad, I'le minister at home,
Such Physick shall content my *Marian.*

Cast. O monstrous ! now the VVorld must see
my shame,
This Head must bear whatever likes my Dame.

Mar. I have no malladie requires cure.

Clin. Why, then must I assume a sick man's
part,   And

And all my sickness lyeth at my heart,
T'is the heart-burning that torments me so.

Marian. There is no cure for fire but to be
quench'd.

Clin. Thou hast prescrib'd a soveraign remedy.

Cast. O who the Devil made her a Physician ?

Clin. Let's not obscure what Love doth ma-
nifest,
Nor let a Stranger's bed make thee seem strange
To him that ever loved and honoured thee.

Mar. A Captain made a Captive by loose
Love,
And gadding Fancie ; fie, 'twere monstrous
shame
That *Cupid's* bow should blemish *Mars* his name;
Take up thy Armes, recall thy drooping
thoughts,
And lead thy Troops into the spacious Fields.

Cast. She counsels others well, if she would
take it.

Clin. Thou counsellest the blinde to lead the
blinde ;
Can I lead them that cannot guide my self ?
Thou, *Marian,* must release my captive Heart.

Mar. With all my heart, I grant thee free release.

Clin. Thou art obscure too much : but tell me,
Love,
Shall I obtain my long-desired Love ?

Mar. Captain, there is yet somewhat in thy
mind
Thou would'st reveal, but wantest utterance;
Thou better knowest to front the braving foe,
Then plead Love suites.

Clin. I grant 'tis even so,
Extremity of passions still are dum.   No

No tongue can tell Love's chief perfections,
Perfwade thy felf my Love-fick thoughts are
    thine,
Thou only mayeft thofe drooping thoughts re-
    fine.
  Mar. Since at my hands thou feek'ft a remedy,
I'le eafe thy grief, and cure thy malady;
No drugg the Doctor hath fhall be too dear,
His antidote fhall flye to do thee good,
Come in and let thy eye make choyfe for thee,
That thou may'ft know how dear thou art to me.
                    Exeunt Clinton, *Marian.*
  Caft. Is this obedience, now the Devil go with
    them,
And yet I dare not; Oh fhe's mankind grown!
O miferable men that muft live fo,
And damned Strumpets, Authors of this woe:
                    Enter Clint. Mar.
But peace! be ftill! they come! O fhamelefs fhame,
Well may the world call thee the Devil's dame.
  Mar. Captain thy skill hath pleafed me fo well,
That I have vowed my fervice to *Bellona.*
  Caft. Her fervice to *Bellona!* turn'd ftark *Ruffian!*
She'le be call'd *Caveleero Marian.*
  Clin. And I will trayn thee up in feats of arms,
And teach thee all the orders of the field,
That whilft we, like to *Mars* and *Venus*, jeft,
The Doctor's head may get a gallant creft.
  Caft. I can no longer linger my difgrace,
Nor hide my fhame from their deteſted fight,
How now thou Whore, dishonour to my bed,
Difdain to Womanhood, fhame of thy fex,
Infatiate monster, corizive of my Soul,
What makes this Captain revelling in my houfe?
My Houfe! nay, in my Bed! you'l prove a Soul
    dier,

I   Follow

Follow *Bellona*, turn a Martialift!
I'le try if thou haft learnt to ward my blowes.
  Mar. Why how now man! is this your mad-
    ding month?
What, fir, will you forbid me in good fort,
To entertain my friends.
  Caft. Your Friends, you Whore:
They are no Friends of mine, nor come they
  Clinton avaunt, my Houfe is for no fuch.   (here:
  Mar. Alafs good fir, are you grown fo fufpici-
Thus on no proofs to nourifh jealoufie;   (ous,
I cannot kiſs a man, but you'l be angry.
In fpite of you, or who fo elfe fayeth nay,
My Friends are welcome as they come this way,
If thou miflike it, mend it as thou may:
VVhat do you think to pin up *Marian*,
As you were wont to do your Spanifh girles,
No fir, I'le be half Miftrifs of my felf,
The other half is yours, if you deferve it.
  Clin. What madnefs mov'd thee be difpleas'd
    with me,
That always us'd thee with fo kind regard,
Did I not at thy firft arrival here
Conduct thee to the Earle of *London's* houfe?
  Mar. Did I not, being unfolicited,
Beftow my firft pure Maiden-love on thee?
  Clin. Did I not grace thee there in all the Court,
And bear thee out againft the daring Abbot?
  Mar. Did I forfake many young Gallant
    Courtiers,
Enamoured with thy aged Gravity?   (me?
Who now being weary of me, would'ft difgrace
  Caft. If there be any Confcience left on earth,
How can I but believe thefe Proteftations?
  Clin. Have I not alwaies been thy neareft
    friend?

Mar.

Mar. Have I not alwaies been thy dearest wife?
Clin. How much will all the world in this
  condemn thee.
Mar. At first I little fear'd what now I find,
And grieve too late.
Caſt. Content thee gentle Dame,
The nature of our Countrymen is ſuch,
That if we ſee another kiſs our Wives,
We cannot brook it: but I will be pleas'd;
For, will I, nill I, ſo me thinks I muſt:
And gentle Captain, be not you offended,
I was too hot at firſt, but now repent it:
I prethee gentle Dame forgive me this,
And drown all iealouſie in this ſweet kiſs.
Clin. This ſhews your wiſdom; on, I'le follow
  you.
Mar. Well Doctor, henceforth never reake it
  ſcorn,
At my ſweet *Clinton's* hands to take the horn.
                                    Exeunt.

ACT. IV.

Enter Robin Good *fellow in a ſuite of Lea-
ther cloſe to his body, his Face and Hands
coloured ruſſet-colour, with a Flayle.*

Rob. The Doctor's ſelf would ſcarce know *Ro-
  bin* now:
Curs't *Marian* may go ſeek another man,
For I intend to dwell no longer with her,
Since that the Baſtinado drove me thence;
Theſe ſilken Girles are all too fine for me,
My Maſter ſhall report of thoſe in Hell,

I 2   Whilſt

Whilſt I go range amongſt the Country maids,
To ſee if home-ſpun Laſſes milder be
Than my curſt Dame, and *Lacie's* wanton wife;
Thus therefore will I live betwixt two ſhapes,
When as I liſt in this transform'd diſguiſe,
I'le fright the Country people as they paſs,
And ſometimes turn me to ſome other form,
And ſo delude them with fantaſtick ſhows:
But woe betide the ſilly Dairy maids,
For I ſhall ſleet their Cream-bowles night by
  night.
And ſlice the Bacon-flitches as they hang.
VVell here in *Croydon* will I firſt begin
To frolick it among the Country Lobs:
This day they ſay is call'd *Holy-rood day*,
And all the Youth are now a nutting gone;
Here are a crew of Yonkers in this VVood,
VVell ſorted, for each Lad hath got his Laſs;
Marrie indeed there is a trickſey Girle,
That three or four would fain be doing with,
But that a wily Prieſt among the reſt,
Intends to bear her there away from all;
The Miller, and my Brother *Grim* the Collier,
Appointed here to ſcuffle for her Love:
I am on *Grim's* ſide, for long time ago
The Devill call'd the Collier like to like:
              Enter Grim, Clack, *Parſon* Shorthoſe,
                        Ioane *with a bagg of Nutts.*
But here the Miller and the Collier come,
VVith Parſon Make-bate, and their trickſey
  Girle.
Grim. Tat'on, perſwade me no more, I come
Iugg to your cuſtody, *Iugg* hold the Nut-bagg.
Clack. Nay, I wil give you Nutts to crack.
Grim. Crack in thy Throat and hauſter too.
Shors. Neighbours I wiſh you both agree.

                                        Let

Let me be judge, be rul'd by me.

Grim. Mr. Parson, remember what *Pluriles*
sayth, *ne accesseris ad consilio*, &c. I tell you I
found this written in the bottom of one of my
empty Sacks; never perswade men that be in-
execrable: I have vowed it, and I will perform
it: the Quarel is great, and I have taken it upon
my own Shou'ders.

Clack. I that thou shalt e're I have done, for I
will lay it on i'faith.

Grim. If you lay it in, I must bear it out: this is
all: if you strike, I must stand to any thing although it be the biggest blow that you can lay
upon me.

Ione. Ye both have oftentimes sworn that ye
love me,
Let me o're-rule you in this angry mood:
Neighbours and old acquaintance, and fall out!

Rob. Why, that is because thou wilt not let them
fall in?

Grim. I say, my heart bleedeth when thou spea-
kest, and therefore do not provoke me: yet Miller, as I am monstrous angry, so I have a wonderfull great mind to be repeas'd: let's think
what harm commeth by this same fighting, if we
should hurt one another, how can we help it?
Again, *Clack*, do but here forswear *Ione's* company, and I'le be thine instead of her, to use in
all your businesses from *Croydon* to *London*, yours
Gilbert Grim, the chief Collier for the King's
Majesties own mouth.

Clack. O *Grim*, do I smell you? I'le make you
forswear her before we two part, and therefore
come on to this geere: Collier I will lay on load,
and when it is done, let who will take it off
again.

I 3   *Iugg.* Yet.

Iugg. Yet once more hear me speak, leave off
for shame,
If not for Love, and let not others laugh,
To see your follies, let me over rule ye,

Short. Oh let them fight, I care not, I,
Mean time away with *Ione* I'le fly,
And whilst they two are at it here,
We two will sport our selves elsewhere.

Rob. There's a stone Priest, he loveth a Wench
indeed,
He careth not though both of them do bleed;
But *Robin Goodfellow* will conjure you,
And marr your match, and bang you soundly,
too;
I like this Country Girle's condition well,
She's faithfull, and a Lover but to one,
Robin stands here to fight both *Grim* and her.

Grim. Master Parson, look you to my Love;
Miller, here I stand with my Heart and my Hand
in sweet *Iugg's* right, with thee to fight.

Clack. Come let us to it then.

They fight, Robin beateth the Miller
with a Flay'e, and felleth him.

Rob. Now Miller, Miller, dustipoule,
I'le clapper-claw your lobbernoule.

Short. Come *Iugg*, lett's leave these sencelesse
Blocks,
Giving each other blowes and knocks.

Ione. I love my *Grim* too well to leave him so.

Short. You shall not choose, come let's away.

Shorthose pulleth Iugg after
him, Robin beateth the Priest
with his Flayle.

Rob. Nay then Sir Priest I'le make you stay.

Clack. Nay this is nothing *Grim*, wel'e not part
so.   I.

I thought to have born it off with my back-
ſword ward, and I receiv'd it vpon my bare
Coſtard. *They fight again.*
Rob. What Miller are you up agin!
Nay then my Flayle ſhall never lin,
Unt'll I force one of us twain,
Betake him to his heels amain.
                    Robin *beats the Miller again.*
Clack. Hold thy hands *Grim,* thou haſt murde-
  red me.
Grim. Thou lyeſt, it is in my own offence I do
it; get thee gone then; I had rather have thy
room than thy company.
Clack. Marry with all my heart; O! the Collier
playeth the Devil with me.
Rob. No, it is the Devil playeth the Collier
  with thee.
Short. My bones are ſore, I prethee *Ione,*
Let's quickly from this place be gone,
Nay come away, I love thee ſo,
Without thee I will never go.
Rob. What Prieſt ſtill at your Lechery,
                    Robin *beats the Prieſt.*
I'le threſh you for your Knavery;
If any ask who beat thee ſo,
Tell them 'twas *Robin Goodfellow.*
                    Short hoſe runneth away.
Grim. Oh Miller art thou gone, I am glad of
it; I ſmell my own infirmity every ſtroke I
ſtruck at him: now *Ione* I dare boldly ſwear thou
art my own, for I have won thee in the plain
field; now Maſter Parſon ſhall even ſtrike it up;
two or three words of his mouth will make her
Gammer *Grim* all the daies of her life after.
Rob. Here is two well-favoured Slaves, *Grim*
  and I may curſe all good faces,
                    I 4   And-

And not hurt our own.
Ione. What, my Love, how doſt thou?
Grim. Even as a Conqueror may do; *Ingg.* for
thy ſake I have made the Miller a poor Criple
all dayes of his life; good for nothing elſe but
to be carried into the ſpittle-houſe.
Rob. I, there is one lye, for thou didſt never
  hurt him.
Ione. I am glad thou ſcapeſt my love, and waſt
  not hurt,
Grim. Who, I hurt! *Ione,* thou knoweſt me
  not yet, thou mayeſt do better hereafter, I
gave him five mortal wounds, the firſt five
ſtrokes I made at him.
Rob. There are five lyes clapt into one for
brevity ſake.
Grim. And preſently upon the fifth blow I
made a dangerous thruſt at him, and vio'ently
overthrew him horſe and foot, and there he
lay.
Rob. Nay, there you lye, the Collier is excellent
To be Companion to the Devil himſelf.
Grim. But where's Maſter Parſon?
Ione. He was well bang'd, and knew not who
  it was did it,
And would have had me gone away with him:
Here lyeth his Nut bag, and the Millers too,
They had no leiſure to take them away.
Grim. The better for us *Ione,* there is good
cracking work, it will increaſe Houſhold-ſtuff:
Come, let's after the Parſon, we will comfort
him, and he ſhall couple us: I'le have *Pounceby*
the Painter ſcore upon our painted Cloath at
home all the whole ſtory of our going a nutting
this *Holy rood-day,* and he ſhall paint me up tri-
                    umphing

This is her evening walk, and here will I
Attend her comming forth, and greet her fairly
  Lacy. See Dunston how their youth doth blind
    our Age,
Thou dost deceive thy self, and bringest me
To see my proper shame and infamy.
                    Enter Honorea.
But here she comes, my hope, my fear, my love,
  Dunst. Here comes the unstained honor of thy
    Bed,
Thy Eares shall hear her vertuous chast replies,
And make thy heare confess thou dost her
    wrong.
  Honorea. Now modest love hath banisht wan-
    ton thoughts,
And altered me from that I was before:
To that chaste life I ought to entertain,
My heart is tyed to that strick't form of life,
That I joy only to be Lacy's wife.
  Lacy. God fill thy minde with these chaste
    vertuous thoughts.
  Musg. Oh now I see her, I am half ashamed,
Of so long absence and neglect of speech;
My dearest Lady, Patroness of Beauty,
Let thy poor Servant make his true excuse.
  Hon. Musgrave, I easely take your excuse,
Accusing my fond self for what is past.
  Musg. Long time we wanted opportunity;
But now the forelock of well wishing time,
Hath blest us both, that here without suspect
We may renew the tenor of our loves.
  Lacy. O Dunstan how she smiles to hear him
    speak !
  Hon. No Childe of fortune and inconstancy,
Thou shalt not traine me, or induce my love
To loose desires, or dishonoured thoughts,
                        This

umphing over the Miller.   Exeunt Grim
                        and Ione.

  Rob So let the Collier now go boast at home
How he hath beat the Miller from his Love;
I like this modest Country-maid so well,
That I believe I must report in hell
Better of women than my Master can:
Well, till my time's expired, I'le keep this Quar-
  ter,
And night by night attend their merry meet-
  ings.   Exit Robin.

  Enter Dunston with Earle Lacy sick.

  Dunston. Let not your sickness adde more
    feebleness
Unto your weakned age, but give me leave
To cure thy vain suspicious malladie.
Thy eyes shall witness how thou art deceived,
Misprizing thy fair Ladies chastity;
For whilst we two stand closely here unseen,
We shall espy them presently approach.
  Lacy O shew me this, thou blessed man of
    God,
And thou shalt then make young my wither'ed
  Age.
  Dunston. Mark the beginning, for here Mus-
    grave commeth.   Enter Musgrave alone.
  Musg. O thrice unhappy and unfortunate,
That having fit occasion profer'd thee
Of conference with beauteous Honorea.
Thou over-slipt it, and o'er-slight tayself;
Never since Wedlock tyed her to the Earle
Have I saluted her, although report
Is blaz'd abroad of my unconstancy.
            I 3.   Thi-

'Tis God's own work that struck a deep re-
morse
Into my tainted heart for my past folly.
Musg. O thou confound'st me, speak as thou
    wert wont,
Like Love herself, my lovely *Honorea.*
    Hon. Why, how now *Musgrave,* what esteem'st
        thou me?
That thou provokest me, that first deny'dst me :
I will not yield you reasons why I may not,
More than your own, you told me why, you
    would not.
    Musg. By Heavens, by thee my Saint, my Hap-
piness,
No torture shall controll my heart in this,
To teach my tongue deny to call thee Love.
    Hon. Well in regard that in my maiden-daies
I lov'd thee well, now let me counsell thee,
Reclaim these idle humors; know thy self,
Remember me; and think upon my Lord;
And let these thoughts bring forth those chaste
    effects,
Which may declare thy change unto the world;
And this assure thee, whilst I breath this aire,
Earle *Lacy's* honour I will ne're impair.
                            Exit Honorea.
    Dunst. Now your Eyes see that which your
        Heart believed not.
    Lacy. It is a miracle beyond the reach
Of my capacitie, I could weep for joy,
Would but my tears express how much I love
    her,
Men may surmise amiss in jealousie,
Of those that live in untouch'd honesty.
    Musg. Is she departed, and do I conceive
This height of grief, and do no violence.
                            Vnto

Vnto my self, said she, I denyed her;
Far be it from my heart to think that thought :
All ye that, as I do, have felt this smart,
Ye know how burdensome 'tis at my heart :
Hereafter never will I prosecute
This former motion, my unlawfull suite :
But since she is Earle *Lacy's* vertuous wife,
I'le live a private pensive single life.   *Ex. Musg.*
    Dunst. God doth dispose all at his blessed will,
And he hath chang'd their minds from bad to
    good,
That we which see't may learn to mend our
    selves.
    Lacy. I'le reconcile my self to *Musgrave's* love,
I will recant my false suspition,
And humbly make my true submission.
                            Exeunt both.

Enter *Marian chasing.*

    Mar. Say'st thou thou'lt make the House too
        hot for me,
I'le soon abroad and cool me in the aire.
I'le teach him never scorn to drink his health
Whom I do love, he thinks to overcrow me
With words and blows, but he is in the wrong,
Begin he when he dares : Oh he's too hot
And angry to live long with *Marian* :
But I'le not long be subject to his rage.
Here 'tis shall rid him of his hatefull life,
And bless me with the stile of Widow hood;
'Twas *Harvey's* work to temper it so well,
The strongest poyson that he could devise.
                            Enter Clinton.

I have been too long subject to the Slave.
                            But

But now I'le cast off that detested yoke.
 Clin. *Musgrave* I see is reconciled to the Eatle,
For now I met him walking with Lord *Lacy*;
Sure this is *Marian's* Plott, and there she stands.
What Love alone!
 Mar. I Captain, much disturb'd
About the frantiek Doctor's jealousie,
Who, though he seemed content when thou
 wast there,
He after fell reviling thee and me,
Rob'd me of all my Jewels, locks his Plate
In his own Trunk, and lets me only live
To bear the idle Title of his Wife.
 Clin. Fair *Marian*, by a Souldier's loyal faith,
If my imployment any way may help
To set thee free from this Captivity,
Vse me in any sort, command my Sword,
I'le do't as soon as thou shalt speak the word.
 Mar. Now by my true Love, whith I wish to
 thee,
I conjure thee with resolution
To slay that Monster, do not fail to do it,
For if thou dost, I would I had not spoke it.
 Clin. Now try me, and when next we hap to
 meet,
The Doctor lies stone dead at *Clinton's* feet,
 Mar. Nay now I see thou lovest me.
 Clin. Say no more;
If thou dost loath him he shall dye therefore.
 Mar. To morrow morning will he early rise
To see Earle *Lacy*, meet him in the Cloyster,
And make that place revenge his Sanctuary!
This night will I break open all the Trunks,
Rifle his Caskets, rob him of his Gold;
And all the Doctors treasure shall be thine,
If thou miscarry, yet this drink shall do it.

 Enter Castil.   *Cast.* My

 Cast. My wive's impatience hath left me alone,
And made my Servant run I know not whither.
 Mar. Peace! here is our eye sore, *Clinton* leave
 us now.
 Clin. Nay now occasion smiles, and I will
 do it.   *Clinton draweth his Sword.*
 Mar. Put up thy Sword; be it thy mornings
 work;
Farewell to night, but fayle me not to morrow.
 Clin. Farewell my Love, no rest shall close
 these eyes;
Vntill the morning peep, and then he dyes.
        Exit Clinton.
 Cast. Now I remember I have quite out-run
My time prefixt to dwell upon the earth;
Yet *Akercock* is absent, where is he:
Oh I am glad I am so well near rid
Of my Earth's plague, and my lascivious dame.
 Mar. Hath he discovered my intendement,
That he presageth his ensuing death?
I must break off these fearfull meditations.
 Cast. How shall I give my verdict up to *Pluto*
Of all these Accidents?
 Mar. Why, how now man!
 Cast. What my dear Dame, my reconciled
 Spouse!
Vpon my Soul, my love to thee is more
Now at this present, than 'twas e're before.
 Mar. He hath discry'd me sure, he sootheth
 me so.
 Cast. I love thee now, because I now must
 leave thee;
This was the day of my Nativity,
And therefore Sweet wife let us revell it.
 Mar. Nay, I have little cause to joy at all,
 Cast. Thou crossest still my Mirth with dis-
 content.   If

If ever heretofore I have displeased thee,
Sweet Dame, I crave thy pardon now for all;
This is my birth day, Girle, I must rejoyce,
Ask what thou wilt, and I will give it thee.
  Mar. Should I but ask to lead a quiet life,
You hardly would grant this unto your wife,
Much less a thing that were of more import.
  Cast. Ask any thing, and try if I'le deny thee.
  Mar. Oh my poor Musgrave, how hast thou
      been wronged,
And my fair Lady!
  Cast. Use no Preambles,
But tell me plainly.
  Mar. Nay remember them,
And joyn their slander to that love you owe me,
And then old Lacye's jealousie
  Cast. What then?
  Mar. Nay now I see you will not understand
      me.
  Cast. Thou art too dark, speak plainly, and
      'tis done.
  Mar. Then doom the Earle, and bless poor
      Musgrave's eyes
With Honorea's love; for this in thy Hand's
      lyes.
  Cast. How should I doom him?
  Mar. How else, but to death?
  Cast. As if his life or death lay in my hands.
  Mar. He is thy Patient, is he not?
  Cast. He is.
  Mar. Then in thy hands lyes both his life
      and death,
Sweet Love, let Marian begg it at thy hands;
Why should the gray beard live to crosse us all?
Nay now I see thee frown; thou wilt not do it.
  Cast. Fy, fy, Dame, you are too suspicious.
                                        Here

Here is my hand, that thou may'st know I love
      thee,
I'le poyson him this night before I sleep.
  Mar. Thou dost but flatter me!
  Cast. Tush, I have sworn it.
  Mar. And wilt thou do it?
  Cast. He is sure to dye.
  Mar. I'le kiss thy Lips for speaking that kind
      word;
But do it, and I'le hang about thy neck,
And curle thy hair, and sleep betwixt thy armes,
And teach thee pleasures which thou never
      knewest.
  Cast. Promise no more, and trouble me no
      more,
The longer I stay here, he lives the longer;
I must go to him now, and now I'le do it:
Go home, and hasten supper 'gainst I come,
We will carrouse to his departing Soul.
  Mar. I will dear Husband, but remember me;
When thou hast poyson'd him, I'le poyson thee.
                                    Ex. Mar.
  Cast. O wonderfull how women can dissemble,
Now she can kiss me, hang about my neck,
And sooth me with smooth smiles and loud in-
      treaties:
Well, I have promis'd her to kill the Earle,
And yet, I hope, ye will not think I'le do it,
Yet I will sound the depth of their device,
And see the issue of their bloody drift,
I'le give the Earle, unknown to any man,
A sleepy potion, which shall make him seem
As if he were stark dead, for certain hours:
But in my absence no man shall report,
That for my Dame's sake I did any hurt.
                                Exit Castiliano.
                                    ACT.

ACT. V.

Enter Grim *with* Ione.

Grim. Nay but *Ione*, have a care, bear a brain
for all at once, 'tis not one hours pleasure that I
suspect, more than your Mother's good countenance; if she be a sleep, we may be bold under
correction, if she be awake, I may go my waies,
and no body ask me, *Grim* whither goest thou:
nay I tell you I am so well beloved in our Town,
that not the worst dogg in the street will hurt
my little finger.

Ione. Why speak you this, you need not fear
my Mother,
For she was fast asleep four hours ago.

Grim. Is she sure, did you hear her snort in
her dead sleep; why then *Ione* I have an hours
mirth for thee.

Ione. And I a mess of Cream for thee.

Grim. Why there is one for another then,
fetch it *Ione*, we will eat and kiss, and be as mer-
Exit Ione *for the Creame.*
ry as your Cricket; art thou gone for for it:
well, go thy waies for the kindest Lass that
ever poor Collier met withall; I mean for to
make short work with her, and marry her presently; I'le single her out i faith, till I make her
bear double, and give the world to understand
we will have a young *Grim* between us.

Enter Ione *with the Creame*

Ione. Look here my Love, 'tis sweetned for thy
mouth. *Grim.* You.

Grim. You have put none of your Love pow-
der in it to make me enamourable of you, have
you *Ione*, I have a simple pate to expect you.
One knocketh at the door.
Ione hark, my Braynes beat, my head works, and
my mind giveth me, some Lovers of yours
come sneaking hither now, I like it not, 'tis
suspectious. *One knocketh again.*

Ione. You need not fear it, for there is none
alive
Shall bear the least part of my heart from thee.

Grim. Sayest thou so, hold there still, and who
e're he be, open door to him.

She openeth the door, enter Shorthose
and Robin *after him.*

Ione. what, Master Parson ! are you come so
late;
You are welcome, here is none but *Grim* and I.

Short. *Ione*, I'le no more a nutting go,
I was so beaten to and fro;
And yet who it was I do not know.

Grim. What, Master Parson, are you come
so late to say evening-song to your Patitioners,
I have heard of your Knavery, I give you a fair
warning, touch her no lower than her Girdle,
and no higher than her chin; I keep her lips
and her hips for my own use; I do, and so welcome.

Rob. This two hours have I dogg'd the Parson round
About all *Croydon*, doubting some such thing.

Short. No Grim, I here foreswear to touch
Thy *Ione*, or any other such;
Love

Love hath been so cudgell'd out of me,
I'le go no more to wood with thee.

Rob. 'Twas *Robin* beat this holy mind into
him,
I think more cudgelling would make him more
honest.

Grim. You speak like an honest man, and a
good Parson, and that is more; here is *Ione*'s be-
nevolation for us, a mess of Cream and so forth.
Here is your place, Master Parson, stand on the
t'other side of the Table *Ione*, eat hard tonight
that thou may marry us the better tomorrow.

Rob. What is my Brother *Grim* so good a
fellow ?   *They fall to the Creame.*
I love a mess of Cream as well as they;
I think it were best I stept in and made one :
Ho, ho, ho my Masters, no good Fellowship !
Is *Robin Goodfellow* a Bug-bear grown.
                         Robin falleth to eat.
That he is not worthy to be bid sit down.

Grim. O Lord save us ! sure he is some Coun-
try-devil, he hath got a Russet-coat upon his
face.

Short. Now *benedicite* ! who is this ?
I take him for some fiend I wiss,
Oh for some holy-water here
Of this same place this Sprite to clear.

Rob. Nay fear not *Grim*, come fall unto your
Creame,
Tut, I am thy Friend, why dost not come and
eat ?

Grim. I Sir, truly, Master Devil, I am well
here, I thank you.

Rob. I'le have thee come, I say, Why trem-
blest thou ?

Grim. No Sir, not I, 'tis a Palsie I have still,
                                      Truly,

Truly, Sir, I have no great acquaintance with
you.

Rob. Thou shalt have better man e're I de-
part.

Grim. I will not, and if I can choose.

Rob. Nay come away, and bring your Love
with you.

Grim. Ione, you were best go to him Ione.

Rob. What shall I fetch the man ? the Cream
is sweet

Grim. No, Sir I am coming; much good do't
you: I had need of a long spoon now I go to eat
with the Devil.

Rob. The Parson's pennance shall be thus to
fast:
Come tell me *Grim*, dost thou not know me
man ?

Grim. No truly Sir, I am a poor man, fetch-
eth my Living out of the fire; your Worship may
be a Gentleman Devil for ought I know.

Rob. Some men call me *Robin Goodfellow*.

Grim. O Lord ! Sir, Mr. *Robert Goodfellow*, you
are very welcome, Sir.

Rob. This half year have I lived about this
Town,
Helping poor Servants to dispatch their work,
To brew and bake, and other Husbandry;
Tut, fear not Maid, if *Grim* be merry,
I will make up the Match between ye

Grim. There will be a Match in the Devil's
name !

Rob. Well now the night is almost spent,
Since your affections all are bent
To Marriage, and to constant Love,
Grim, Robin doth thy Choyse approve,
And there's the Priest shall marry you;

                                      G2

Go to it, and make no more ado:
Sirrah, Sir Priest, go get you gone,
And joyn both her and him anon;
But ne're hereafter let me take you
With wanton Love-tricks, lest I make you
Example to all stone-priests ever,
To deal with other mens loves never.

Short. Valete vos, and God bless me,
And rid me from his Company.
Come *Grim* I'le joyn you hand in hand,
In sacred Wedlock's holy band;
I will no more a nutting go,
That journey caused all this woe.

Grim. Come, let's to hand in hand quickly,
Master *Robert* you were ever one of the honestest
merry Devils that ever I saw.

Ione. Sweet *Grim*, and if thou lovest me let's
away.

Grim. Nay, now *Ione*, I spy a hole in your coat,
if you cannot endure the Devil, you'l never
love the Collier, why we two are sworn Bro-
thers, you shall see me talk with him even as
familiarly as if I should parbreak my mind and
my whole stomach upon thee.

Ione. I prethee do not *Grim*.

Grim. Who, not I? O Lord! Mr. *Robert Goodfellow*, I have a poor Cottage at home, whither
Ione and I will jog as merrily; we will make you
no Stranger if you come thither, you shall be u-
sed as devilishly as you would wish i'faith; there
is never a time my Cart commeth from *London*,
but the Collier bringeth a Goose in his Sack and
that, with the Giblets thereof, is at your service.

Rob. This is more kindness *Grim* than I ex-
pected.

                              Grim. Nay.

Grim. Nay, Sir, if you come home, you shall
find it true I warrant you, all my whole Family
shall be at your Devilships pleasure, except my
poor *Ione* here, and she is my own proper night
geer.

Rob. Gramercies, but away in hast,
The night is almost spent and past.

Grim. God be with you, Sir, I'le make as
much hast about it as may be, for and that were
once done, I would begin a new piece of work
with you *Ione*.

                    Exeunt all but Robin.

Rob. Now joy betide this merry morn,
And keep *Grims* forehead from the horn,
For *Robin* bids his last adieu,
To *Grim* and all the rest of you.   *Ex.* Rob.

            Enter Clinton *alone.*

Clin. Bright *Lucifer* go cochw thee in the Clouds,
And let this morning prove as dark as night,
That I unseen may bring to happy end
The Doctor's murder, which I do intend:
It's early yet, he is not so soon stirring;
But stir he ne're so soon, so soon he dies;
I'le walk along before the Pallace gate;
Then shall I know how near it is to day,
He shall have no means to escape away.
                              Exit Clinton.

            Enter Castiliano.

Cast. My Trunk's broke open, and my Iewels
        gone,
My Gold and Treasure stolne, my House dis-
spoyl'd
                                        of

Of all my Furniture, and nothing left,
No no: my Wife, for she is stoln away,
But she hath pepper'd me, I feel it work,
My Teeth are loose, and my Belly swell'd,
My Entrails burn with such distemper'd heat,
That well I know my Dame hath poyson'd me;
When she spoke fairest, then she did this Act.
When I have spoken all I can imagine,
I cannot utter half that she intends;
She makes as little poysoning of a man
As to carrouse, I feel that this is true:

Enter Clinton.

Nay now I know too much of Women kind,
Zoun's here's the Captain! what should he make
    here
With his Sword drawn? there's yet more Vil-
    lany.

Clin. The morning is far spent, but yet he
    comes not!
I wonder *Marian* sends him not abroad!
Well Doctor, linger time and linger life,
For long thou shalt not breath upon the earth.

Cast. No, no, I will not live amongst ye long,
Is that for me thou waitest thou bloody Wretch?
Her Poyson hath prevented thee in Murther.

Enter Earle Morgan, *St.* Dunston, *with*
Honorea *fainting*, *and* Mariana.

Now here be they suppose Earle *Lacy* dead,
See how his Lady grieveth for that she wisheth?
Dunst. My Lord of *London*, by his sudden death,
And all the signs before his late departure,
'Tis very probable that he is poyson'd.
Marian. Do you but doubt it! credit me my
    Lord,
I heard him say, That drink should be his last,
                                I heard

I heard my Husband speak it, and he did it.
Cast. There is my old Friend, she alwaies
    speaks for me;
Oh shameless Creature! was't not thy devise?
Morg. Let not extremity of grief o'rewhelme
My dearest *Honorea*, for his death shall be (thee,
Surely reveng'd with all severity
Upon the Doctor, and that suddenly.
Clin. What Fortune's this, that all these come
To hinder me, and save thy life to day. (this way
Hon. My gracious Lord, this dolefull accident
Hath rob'd me of my joy; And royal Earle,
Though in thy life thou did'st suspect my love,
My grief and tears suspicions shall remove.
Mar. Madam to you and to your Father's
I owe as much & more than my own life, (love,
Had I ten Husbands should agree to do it,
My gracious Lord you presently should know it.
Cast. I! there's a Girle: Think you I did not well
To live with such a Wife, to come from Hell.
Mar. Look, look, my Lord, there stands the
    Murderer.
Cast. How am I round beset on every side!
First, that same Captain, here stands to kill me,
My Dame she hath already poysoned me,
Earle *Morgan* he doth threaten present death,
The Countess *Honorea*, in revenge
Of *Lacy*, is extremely incens'd against me;
All threatens, none shall do it, for my date
Is now expired, and I must back to Hell.
And now my Servant wheresoe're thou be,
Come quick'ly *Akercock*, and follow me;
Lordings adieu, and my curst Wife farewell,
If me ye seek, come follow me to Hell.
    The Ground opens, and he falls down into it.
Morg. The Earth that opened, now is clos'd
    again!   *Dun.* It

Dunst. It is God's judgement for his grievous
life.
Clo. Was there a Quagmire, that he sunk so
soon?
Hon. O miracle! now may we justly say,
Heavens have reveng'd my Husband's death
this day.
Morg. Alas poor *Marian!* we have wrong'd
thee much.
To couple thee match thy self to any such.
Mar. Nay let him go, and sink into the ground,
For such as he are better lost then found;
Now *Honorea* we are fre'd from blame,
And both enrich'd with happy Widows names.

Enter Earl Lacy *with* Forest, Musgrave.

Lacy O lead me quickly to that mourning train,
Which weep for me, that am revived again.
Hon. *Marian,* I shed some tears of perfect grief.
She falleth into a Sound.
Morg. Do not my Eyes deceive me? liveth my
Son?
Lacy. My Lord, and Father, both alive and
well
Recovered of my weakness: where's my wife?
Mar. Here is my Lady, your beloved wife,
Half ceas'd to hear of your untimely end.
Lacy. Look on me, *Honorea;* see thy Lord:
I am not dead, but live to love thee still.
Dun. 'Tis God disposeth all things as he will;
He raiseth those, the wicked wish to fall.
Win. Zounds, I still watch on this inclosed
For if he rise again, I'le murder him, (ground;
Hon. My Lord, my tongue's not able to report
Those joys my heart conceives to see thee live?

K   *Dun.* Give:

Dunst. Give God the glory; he recovered thee,
And wrought this judgement on that cursed
man,
That set debate and strife among ye all.
Morg. My Lord, our eyes have seen a miracle,
Which after-ages ever shall admire,
The Spanish Doctor, standing here before us,
Is sunk into the bowels of the earth,
Ending his vile life by a viler death.
Lacy. But, gentle *Marian,* I bewail thy loss,
That wer't Maid, Wife, and Widow, all so soon.
Mar. 'Tis your recovery that joys me more
Than grief can touch me for the Doctor's death;
He never lov'd me whilst he liv'd with me,
Therefore the less I mourn his Tragedy.
Morg. Henceforth we'l strictlier look to
Strangers lives,
Now they shall marry any English Wives:
Now all men shall record this fatal day,
Lacy revived, the Doctor sunk in Clay.
*The Trumpets sound, exeunt all
but* Dunstan.
Dunst. Now is Earl *Lacy*'s House fill'd full of
He and his Lady wholy reconcil'd,   (joy,
Their jars all ended; those that were like men
Transformed, turn'd unto their shapes again:
And Gentlemen, before we make an end,
A little longer yet your patience lend,
That in your friendly censures you may see
What the infernal synod do decree,
And after judge, if we deserve to name
This Play of ours, *The Devil and his Dame.* Exit.
It thunders and lightneth; enter Pluto, Minos, Æacus, Rhadamanthus, *with Furies
bringing in* Malbecco's *ghost.*

Pluto

Pluto. Minos, Is this the day he should return
And bring us tidings of his Twelve month
spent.

> *Enter* Belphagor *like a Devil, with*
> *Horns on his head, and* Akerkok.

Minos. It is, great King, and here *Belphagor*
comes.

Pluto. His Visage is more ghastly than it was
wont.

What Ornaments are those upon his head?

Bel. Hell, I salute thee, now I feel my self
Rid of a thousand torments; O vile Earth,
Worse for us Devils, then Hell it self for men!
Dread *Pluto*, hear thy Subject's just Complaint.

> *Belph.* kneeleth to *Pluto.*

Proceeding from the anguish of my Soul,
O never send me more into the Earth,
For there dwells dread, and horror more then
here.

Pluto. Stand forth *Belphagor*, and report the
truth.
Of all things have betide thee in the World.

Bel. When first, great King, I came into the
Earth,
I chose a Wife both young and beautifull,
The only Daughter to a noble Earl:
But when the night came, that I should her bed,
I found another laid there in her stead,
And in the morning when I found the change,
Though I deny'd her, I was forc'd to take her;
With her I lived in such a milde estate,
Used her still kindly, loved her tenderly;
Which she requited with such light regard,
So loose demeanour, and dishonest life,
That she was each man's whore that was my wife:

K2 NO

No hours but Gallants flock'd unto my house,
Such as she fancied for her loathsome lust,
With whom, before my face, she did not spare
To play the Strumpet; yea, and more than this,
She made my house a stue for all resorts,
Herself a Bawd to other's filthiness;
Which if I once began but to reprove,
Oh! then her Tongue was worse than all the rest,
No ears with patience would endure to hear her,
Nor would she ever cease till I submit,
And then she would speak me fair, but wish me
A hundred drifts she laid to cut me off,   (dead:
Still drawing me to dangers of my life;
And now my Twelve-month being near expir'd,
She poysoned me; and least that means should
She entic'd a Captain to have murdered me (fail,
In brief, whatever Tongue can tell,
All that may well be spoken of my Dame.

Aker. Poor *Akerkok* was fain to fly her sight,
For ne're an hour but she laid on me,
Her Tongue and Fist walked all so nimblely.

Pluto. Doth then *Belphagor* this report of thine
Against all Women hold in general?

Bel. Not so, great Prince, for as 'mongst other
Creatures,
Under that Sex are mingled good and bad,
There are some women vertuous, chast and true,
And to all those the Devil will give their due:
But, Oh my Dame! born for a song to man,
For no mortality would endure that,
Which she a thousand times hath offered me.

Pluto. But what new shapes are those upon thy
Head?

Bel. These are the ancient arms of Cuckoldry,
And these my Dame hath kindly left to me,
For which *Belphagor* shall be here derided,

Vnless

Vnlesse your great infernal Majestie
Do solemnly proclaime, no devil shall scorn
Hereafter still to wear the goodly horn
That this for thy service will grant thee freely,
All Devils shall, as thou dost like horns wear,
And none shall scorn *Belphagor's* armes to bear ;
And now *Malbecco*, hear thy latest doom,
Since that thy first Reports are justified
By after-proofs, and Women's loosenesse known,
One Plague more will I send upon the earth,
Thou shalt assume a light and fiery shape,
And so for ever live within the world.
Dive into Womens thoughts, into mens hearts,
Raise up false rumours, and suspicious fears,
Put strange inventions into each man's mind ;
And for these Actions they shall alwaies call thee
By no name else but fearfull Iealousie :
Go Iealousie, be gone, thou hast thy charge,
Go range about the World that is so large.
And now for joy *Belphagor* is return'd,
The Furies shall their tortures cast away,
And in Hell wee will make it Holy-day.

                    It thundereth and lighteneth,
                         exeunt omnes.

FINIS.

Lightning Source UK Ltd.
Milton Keynes UK
UKOW05f1024180917
309396UK00007B/537/P